Debbie Shore's
SEWING ROOM SECRETS
Essential skills
for dressmakers

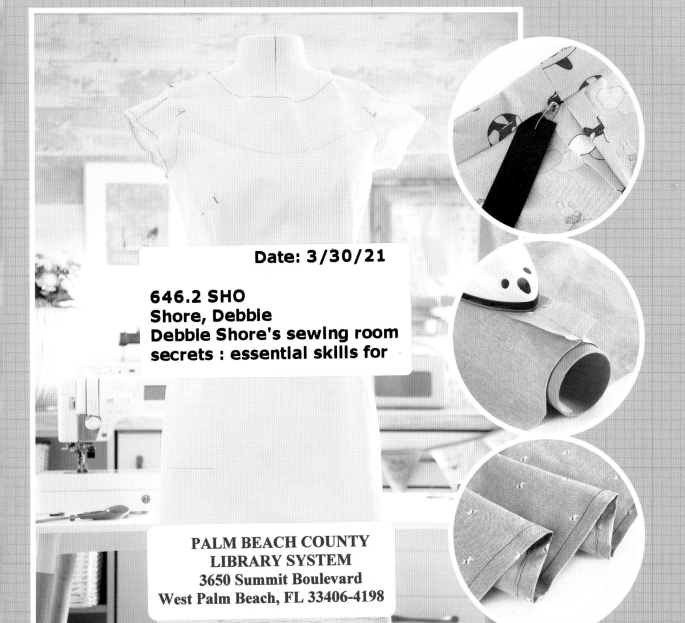

First published in 2021

Search Press Limited
Wellwood, North Farm Road,
Tunbridge Wells, Kent TN2 3DR

Photographs by Garie Hind
Models: Kimberley Hind, Beatrix Kaley and Vienna-Rae Aramanda

ISBN: 978-1-78221-747-3
ebook ISBN: 978-1-78126-703-5

The Publishers and author can accept no responsibility for any
consequences arising from the information, advice or instructions
given in this publication.

Readers are permitted to reproduce any of the items/patterns in
this book for their personal use, or for the purposes of selling for
charity, free of charge and without the prior permission of the
Publishers. Any use of the items/patterns for commercial purposes
is not permitted without the prior permission of the Publishers.

The projects in this book have been made using metric measurements,
and the imperial equivalents provided have been calculated following
standard conversion practices. The imperial measurements are often
rounded to the nearest $1/8$in for ease of use. If you need more exact
measurements, there are a number of excellent online converters
that you can use. Always use either metric or imperial measurements,
not a combination of both.

Suppliers
For details of suppliers, please visit the Search Press website:
www.searchpress.com

For further inspiration:
– join the Half Yard Sewing Club: www.halfyardsewingclub.com
– visit Debbie's YouTube channel: www.youtube.com/user/thimblelane
– visit Debbie's website: www.debbieshoresewing.com

Debbie Shore's
SEWING ROOM SECRETS
Essential skills
for dressmakers

SEARCH PRESS

CONTENTS

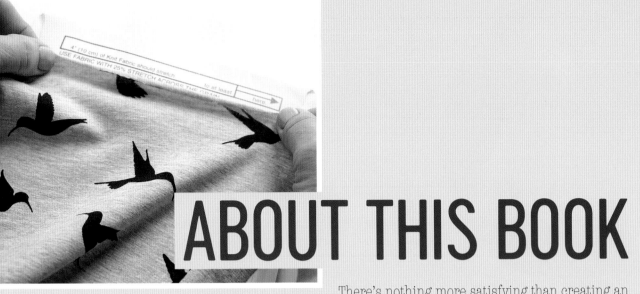

ABOUT THIS BOOK

There's nothing more satisfying than creating an outfit in a fabric of your choice that fits you just right! Many of us would like to make our own clothes but find the idea a bit daunting: pattern instructions, markings, fitting and the thought of making that first cut into beautiful fabric can be quite off-putting. In this book, I hope to demystify the jargon to give you the confidence to have a go!

But of course you don't have to start from scratch – we'll look at altering garments you already have, upcycling garments you're no longer fond of or have bought from charity and thrift shops, and extending the life of your wardrobe by mending and repairing instead of throwing away worn-out garments.

Dressmaking doesn't have to be an expensive business; for instance, fabric doesn't have to be bought from fabric stores – some real bargains can be found on auction websites, and it's worth looking for end of lines and items that you can re-purpose.

Start simple – don't get hung up on 'perfection', instead just wait for the best compliment any dressmaker can receive: 'where did you buy that?' (Usually followed by 'can you make me one?')

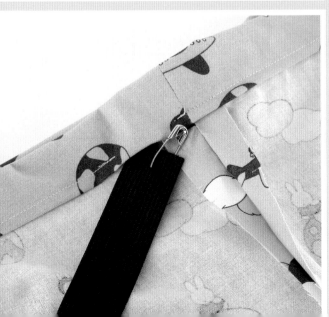

ABOUT ME

My mum was a seamstress, making clothes for me, my sister and other members of the family, particularly when a wedding was forthcoming! Our house was always busy with fittings, the drawers and cupboards were filled with fabrics and the sound of sewing machines revving and crisp scissors crunching through layers of fabric is still very nostalgic for me. Sewing was never my intended career, more of a hobby and necessity, particularly when I had kids of my own and alterations and repairs were the affordable way of keeping their wardrobes smart and up-to-date!

For over thirty years I have worked as a TV presenter, while still enjoying my sewing hobby in my spare time. A few years ago, several elements of my life started coming together… I was making up some cushion covers which I was so pleased with I asked my husband Garie, a fashion photographer, to take some pictures. I sent the projects off to Search Press, who produced my first book, *Making Cushion Covers.* This was the first of now 23 sewing project books, and my own range of patterns and products, which I present on shopping TV.

So now my own cupboards are filled with fabrics and my home has the sound of revving sewing machines and crunching scissors. Who knows, in a few years' time my children may be saying exactly the same thing!

MY QUICK TIPS

A few key dressmaking tips before you get started…

- Always read the instructions! Pattern manufacturers may use different terms and have different seam allowances, so make sure you understand the pattern before cutting into your fabric.

- Allow the thread to run off the top of the spool whether machine or hand sewing – it will help stop the thread twisting.

- Make a toile (see page 39)! It's worth the extra time to make sure your garment fits perfectly – any alterations can be made to the pattern before cutting into your final fabric.

- Invest in a lint roll, particularly if you're working with fabrics like corduroy and fleeces, which tend to be magnets for dust, threads and cat hair!

- Stick a tape measure along the front of your cutting table – it's a handy way to measure fabrics.

- If you find your foot slips off your sewing machine pedal, wrap a couple of elastic bands around it to give it a bit of grip.

- Not sure which is the right side of a plain fabric? Take a look at the selvedge/selvage. The hooks that stretch the fabric in the printing process go through the edges of the fabric from the back to front, so the front side will have little holes that appear rougher than the back.

- Mark an accurate seam allowance by tying together two pencils. The distance between the two points will be 5mm (¼in). Pop another pencil in the middle and you'll have a 1.5cm (⅝in) seam allowance – the most commonly used seam allowance when dressmaking.

- Toe separators are a perfect place for storing bobbins!

- Sewing a straight line? Practice makes perfect. In the meantime, use the markings on the needle plate, or try putting masking tape or an elastic band over the bed of your machine and using this as a guide for the edge of your fabric.

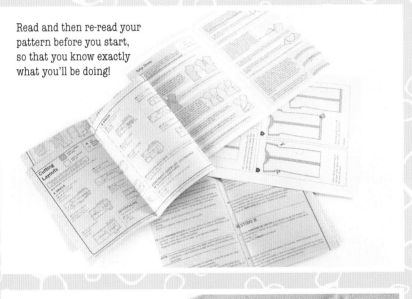

Read and then re-read your pattern before you start, so that you know exactly what you'll be doing!

Make a toile to test out your pattern using cheaper fabric (see page 39).

Selvedges/selvages tell you which side is the front of the fabric.

DRESSMAKING
ESSENTIALS

TOOLS & EQUIPMENT

When it comes to dressmaking, there are tools that you'll *need* and tools that you may just rather *like*. For example, you'll need a sewing machine; you may like an expensive all-singing-all-dancing model but that's not really necessary. You may also like an overlocker/serger, and although they're really useful, you can easily create garments without one. It's wonderful to have an armoury of scissors but you can get by with three pairs. So I've split this chapter into 'tools you need' and 'tools you might like', depending on your budget!

TOOLS YOU NEED

Sewing machine

I'd recommend buying a computerized machine from a big-name brand (see top image, opposite). Computerized machines are generally a bit more expensive than electronic machines but are easier to use and have a wider stitch selection. For dressmaking, look for a machine with a needle up/down facility – the needle will automatically stop in the down position, so if you stop sewing halfway along your seam, the stitch line will carry on precisely when you resume sewing.

Some machines can be used without the foot pedal, making sewing possible for those of you who can't use your feet, or prefer to sew standing at a high counter where the pedal won't reach the floor. These machines will have a speed control, which can be used either with or without the pedal – a bonus for those who are nervous about how quickly the machine is sewing!

There are a few other features that I consider invaluable: I would never buy a machine without a needle threader, as I've wasted so much time trying to thread needles by hand! And a one-step buttonhole stitch is so much simpler than a four-step: the buttonhole presser foot measures the size of the button, making all the buttonholes uniform in size, and the machine will automatically stop when the buttonhole is finished.

Big brands tend to offer longer warranties and support – this will give you peace of mind when you're spending a lot of money on a sewing machine – you want it to last for years!

Finally, read reviews: many online retailers have star systems and show both good and bad experiences from other customers.

Sewing-machine feet

Your machine will probably come with all the feet you need to get started; if you need extra feet they should be available from your manufacturer or dealer. I must confess, I rarely change from my standard foot, even when sewing zips! However, I will change it if I'm blind or roll hemming, quilting or free-motion sewing (these sewing-machine feet can be found in the 'tools you might like' section on page 17).

A standard foot is suitable for most projects – it's the foot that will be on your machine when it arrives. The look of the foot may be different from one manufacturer to another, but it will basically allow you to sew any stitch on your machine.

A zipper foot allows the needle to get close to the zip teeth, and is also useful for making piping.

Sewing-machine needles

Needles are sized in metric and imperial. The smaller the number the finer the needle, and the size of a needle is calculated by its diameter; for example an 80 needle is 0.8mm in diameter. Understanding needles and their associated numbers will help you to make the correct choice for your fabric and thread, resulting in perfect seams.

These are my most-used needles:

Size 10/70 organza, silk
Size 11/75 lingerie, satin
Size 12/80 taffeta, quilt cotton, lining fabric, voile, jersey
Size 14/90 jeans and heavy cotton, linen
Size 16/100 velvet, lace
Size 18/110 wool, upholstery fabric, faux leather, laminates, twill
Size 20/120 thick denim, canvas, heavy faux leather

A denim needle isn't just for denim; it's a strong needle with a very sharp point, making it suitable for thick fabrics.

A stretch or ball-point needle has a slightly rounded tip, allowing it to part the threads of knitted fabric such as jersey, instead of tearing through it. Sewing stretch fabric with a regular needle can result in skipped stitches.

A metallic needle has an elongated eye that allows metallic threads to pass through with minimal friction.

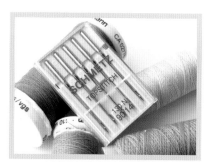

A topstitch needle has an extra-large eye to accommodate thick threads.

An embroidery needle has a long groove and large eye, which allows delicate embroidery threads to pass through easily and reduce friction.

A universal needle can be used on knit or woven fabrics, so these will be your go-to needles if you're not sure of the fibre content of your fabric. It's so frustrating if you need a new needle halfway through a project and you don't have any in your sewing kit, so invest in a few packets!

A leather needle has an angled point that makes a tiny slit instead of a round hole, to help the thread pass smoothly through leather, suede and imitations.

A twin needle

A twin needle is constructed of two needles that are joined with one shank, which fits into the needle holder on your sewing machine in the same way as your standard needle. When using a straight stitch, you'll see two rows of stitches on the top, while underneath the single thread from the bobbin zigzags from one row of stitches to the other, making this a perfect way to hem stretch fabrics.

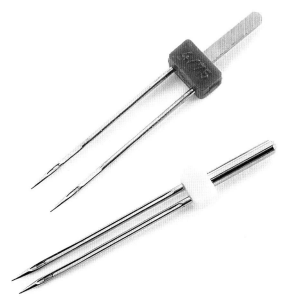

Twin needles come in sizes from 1.6mm to 6mm, which is the distance between the two needles. The wider needles are more suited to hemming. If you're using stretch fabric then make sure you use a twin stretch needle, as these have slightly rounded points to help prevent tearing the threads in the fabric.

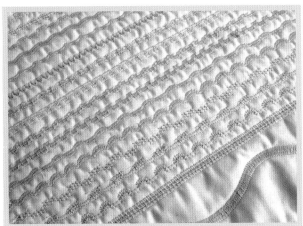

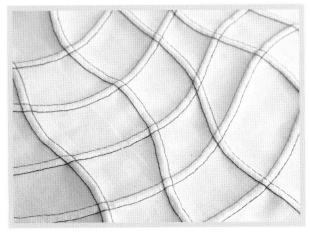

Pass both top threads through the normal channels until you reach the needles, then thread each individually by hand (your needle threader won't work with a twin needle). Many sewing machines will have a selection button for twin-needle sewing, preventing you from using unsuitable stitches such as buttonholes. If you're using a decorative stitch and you don't have this function, test the stitch first by turning the hand wheel slowly, to make sure that the needles don't hit the sides of the foot as they swing from side to side. If the stitch is too wide this could result in broken needles!

Always practise on a scrap piece of fabric first, as some decorative stitches work better than others.

Use a grooved pin-tucking foot in combination with your twin needle to create pin tucks to decorate blouses, dresses or pillow covers. The grooves in the presser foot act as guides for parallel sewing. You may need to increase the tension on your sewing machine to create a raised area of fabric between the lines. Cord can be used under the rows of stitches to raise them even more. And remember, there's nothing to say that pin tucks must be sewn in straight lines!

Scissors and shears

Scissors have symmetrical handles allowing you to use one finger and your thumb; shears have a larger handle to fit all of your fingers, which is angled to enable the cutting blade to sit flat on your fabric, preventing the fabric from lifting too much as you're cutting.

You'll need a good pair of dressmaking shears. They come with many lengths of blade – the measurement is from the tip of the blade to the back of the finger hole. I find 23cm (9in) shears a useful size.

You'll need a small pair of sharp scissors for snipping threads or into corners.

Finally, you'll need scissors for cutting paper. I'll occasionally cut tissue paper patterns with my dressmaking shears, but it's good practice to use your fabric scissors and shears just to cut fabric and paper scissors just to cut paper, as paper can eventually blunt the blades.

Tape measure

Choose a plastic measure as it won't stretch, with both metric and imperial measurements so that you're covered no matter where your pattern comes from!

Seam ripper/quick unpick

One of these will come with your sewing machine, but seam rippers eventually blunt so it's useful to have a few. We all make wonky stitches occasionally!

Pins

If you're using a fine fabric, pin into the seam allowance around the edge of the pattern so you don't leave holes in the material.

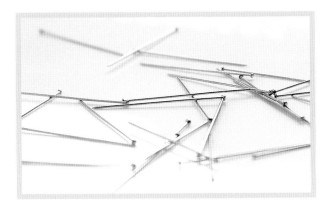

Dressmakers' pins are long, fine steel pins with small heads.

I prefer to use glass-headed pins as I can see them easily and find them easier to pick up!

Safety pins

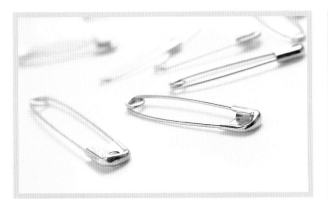

Threading elastic through a casing is easily done by attaching a safety pin to one end to give you something to grip; attach the other end of the elastic to the fabric with another safety pin to prevent the elastic disappearing into the casing!

Hand-sewing needles

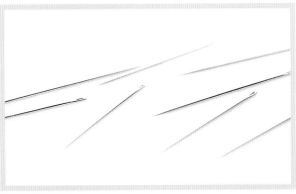

There's always a time to use a hand-sewing needle, even when most of your garment is made on the machine – for instance, sewing interfacing into a seam to keep it flat. There are no rules here – I like to use sharps, which are long, slim needles with a round eye, as they are good for hand sewing most projects.

Pincushion

To keep pins and needles all in one place, you'll need a pincushion. A magnetic pincushion is useful for picking up dropped pins.

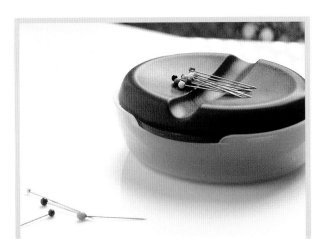

Marking tools

You'll need to transfer markings from your pattern to your fabric and there are many ways to do this.

Chalk is an easy option and is available in many colours – choose at least one light and one dark so they stand out on your fabric no matter what colour it is. Chalk triangles (above left) are traditionally used, but chalk wheels (above centre) are now available and create fine, accurate lines.

Dressmakers' carbon paper comes in a variety of colours, and is used with a tracing wheel on the wrong side of your fabric. I find this the quickest way to transfer markings accurately. If your fabric is on the fold you'll need to flip over the pattern to transfer markings to both sides. Adjustable double wheels are also available to help you mark the perfect seam allowance!

Air-erasable ink disappears after a few hours (check the manufacturer's guidelines), while water-erasable ink dissolves when wet. Be warned though: if these inks are ironed they will become permanent!

Heat-erasable pens aren't really meant for use with fabric and may stain or bleach it, so do a patch test first or just use within the seam allowance.

French curve

This curved ruler makes pattern adjustments easier when grading patterns, particularly around armholes and hips. French curves come in a variety of sizes, with both metric and imperial measurements.

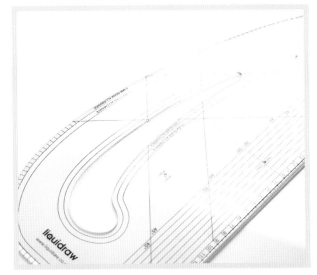

Iron

Use an iron with controllable heat settings, with or without steam. I use a steam generator iron that I can happily leave on for an hour or so until it automatically switches off. Pressing seams and hems, and creating folds and creases where needed, are crucial in the dressmaking process and will improve the look of your garments (see page 27).

Tailors' ham

It's impossible to press a three-dimensional shape on a flat surface, so a tailors' ham, stuffed with sawdust to absorb steam, makes a perfect pressing surface for shoulders and darts. You'll also find one useful if you venture into bag making. A rolled-up towel makes a handy alternative.

TOOLS YOU MIGHT LIKE

Advanced sewing machine

Generally, the more you spend on a machine, the more stitches and features it will have. My machine has over 150 stitches, but you can find machines with many more! Some feature alphabet stitches so that you can personalize your work, some combine sewing with embroidery, while others have WiFi capability to transfer designs straight from your PC. The sky is the limit! Do think carefully about what you actually need from your machine before spending a fortune though, as there's little point in spending thousands on a machine if you're not going to use its capabilities. It's a good idea to buy from a store where you can 'test drive' the machine first and, as with any machine, make sure you have suitable warranties and manufacturer support in place.

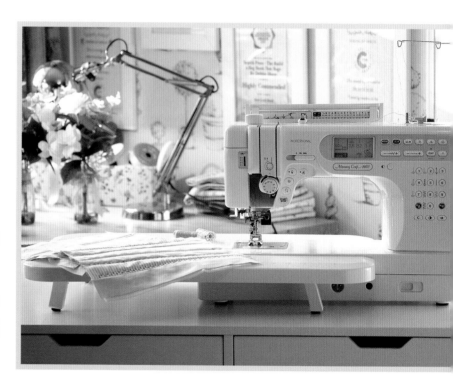

16

Sewing-machine feet

There are many more feet available than the ones I feature here, but these are the ones I think will make your dressmaking journey a bit easier.

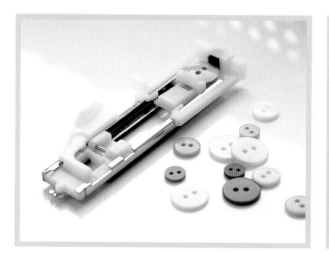

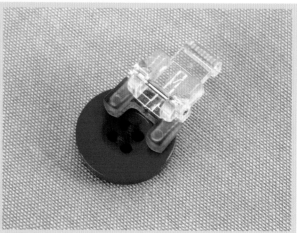

A buttonhole foot is used for sewing buttonholes (above left); a button placement foot is useful for sewing buttons on (above right).

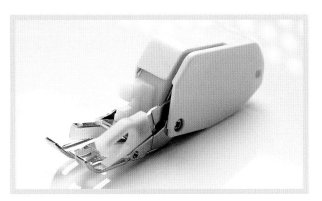

A walking, or even-feed, foot has 'teeth' that work with the feed dogs to feed layers of fabric through the machine from the top at the same rate as the feed dogs underneath. It's especially useful if you're sewing slippery or stretch fabrics, which may distort as you sew, and it's also great for laminated fabrics or when sewing multiple layers, as with quilting. Take the ankle off your machine, then screw the foot to the take-up lever with the 'claw' wrapped around the needle clamp.

Although it is possible to fit an invisible or concealed zip with a regular zipper foot, a concealed zip foot opens out the coil of the zip as you sew, making accurate stitching a breeze! (See also page 57.)

When sewing faux leathers or laminates, your regular presser foot can prevent the fabric flowing freely under the needle; a non-stick foot prevents this dragging by allowing the fabric to glide.

An overcast/overedge foot allows the stitch to be taken over the edge of the fabric, so when used with an overcast stitch, it gives an overlocked/serged look to finish seams and stop them from fraying.

A blind-hem foot is used with the blind-hem stitch on your machine. This foot has a guide that is sometimes adjustable, which ensures the stitches are in the correct position when sewing a hem.

A rolled-hem foot guides the fabric through a small 'roll', which turns it over twice to create a very narrow hem. This is the perfect foot for use with fine fabrics or for hemming curves.

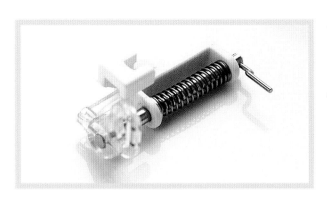

A free-motion/darning/embroidery foot is not just for quilters, as free-motion embroidery can be used to decorate and mend holes in clothing (see page 92). Drop the feed dogs (or cover them over) to allow you to move the fabric in any direction you like under the needle. This foot has a spring to allow the foot to 'hop' over the fabric, while the bar at the top of the foot sits over the needle clamp to help it bounce!

Overlocker/serger

An overlocker/serger is a good investment if you're planning on doing a lot of dressmaking. It is fast – an overlocker/serger can sew twice as fast as a domestic sewing machine – and is ideal for finishing seams or for use with stretch fabrics.

Thread is bought on cones, and the machines can use three, four or five cones at a time. I'd recommend a four-thread overlocker/serger (these can also use three cones). Use three threads for lightweight fabric to create a less bulky, flat seam, and four threads for strength. Five-thread overlockers are quite expensive but do create a strong seam for heavy-weight fabrics. The combination of needle and looper thread takes the stitch over the edge of the fabric, followed swiftly by a blade that chops off excess seam allowance. Threading an overlocker isn't as complicated as it may look, but to make life easier you could invest in an air-thread machine where the looper threads are pushed into position through narrow tubes with blasts of air.

Most machines have the capability to create a rolled hem by using three threads and disengaging the blade, creating neat, narrow hems. Some also have a differential feed which can create a ruffled effect or stretch the fabric to create a frill, depending on the speed it is set at.

An overlocker/serger won't replace your sewing machine but will certainly work well alongside it.

Seam guide

Available with metric or imperial measurements, these tools are small and convenient measuring aids. Simply slide the marker over the edge of your fabric and mark where required – so much easier than using a tape measure!

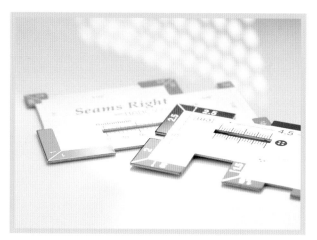

Heat-resistant rulers

These nylon-fibre boards can withstand the heat of an iron and are non-slip. Fold your fabric around the ruler and iron; some will allow you to make neat mitred corners or neat curves around patch pockets.

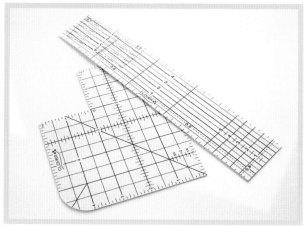

Buttonhole cutter

You may wish to buy a buttonhole cutter if you're making lots of buttonholes, as they allow you to cut accurately without fraying the fabric. These act like a chisel, with a sharp blade at one end that you place onto the fabric; tap the handle with a hammer to cut the hole in the fabric. They are available in different sizes, but a small cutter can be moved along the hole to widen it. Use a block of wood underneath so you don't damage your table!

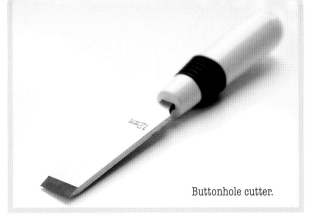

Buttonhole cutter.

Pinking shears

These shears cut fabric with small 45-degree zigzags, preventing it from fraying. They are an easy way to finish seams, snip around curves where necessary or reduce bulk in seams.

Pinking shears.

Rotary cutter and mat

If you have a steady hand you may prefer to cut around patterns with a rotary cutter – the benefit is that your fabric is kept flat, and slippery or stretch fabrics are less likely to distort. A 45mm rotary blade is the most used size; you'll find a 28mm blade useful for cutting around small areas of a pattern. You'll also need a large cutting mat so that you don't have to move the pattern about as you're cutting.

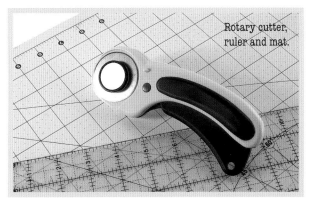

Rotary cutter, ruler and mat.

Hemming tools

Seam gauges are available with metric or imperial measurements, helping you to accurately measure seams and hems. Some come with a small wheel that enables you to draw curves and circles!

Dress form

A dress form can be really useful if you have one that fits your measurements – getting an adjustable dress form means that if you're making a garment for someone else you can fit the garment without the customer being present. If a dress form doesn't match your figure it can be padded out but, to be honest, if you're making for yourself it will be more affordable to just fit your garment to your body!

Dress form.

Seam gauges.

FABRICS

The colour and print of your fabric is entirely your choice, but do buy the *type* of fabric recommended on your pattern – the designer knows which fabric type will work best. There are so many fabrics available nowadays that it can be a bit overwhelming, so I've picked out some of the most used in dressmaking.

FABRIC BUYING TIPS

- If you're a beginner, choose a woven fabric that won't slip as you sew it; avoid slippery or stretchy fabrics until you're more confident.
- Consider your print: plain fabrics will make darts stand out and large prints, stripes and large checks may need pattern matching. On the other hand, small prints can help to disguise wobbly stitches...
- Try to buy from a store if you have one locally – you'll be able to hold the fabric against your skin to make sure the colour suits you, feel the drape of the fabric, and ask advice from the knowledgeable staff if you need help with working out the quantity you require.

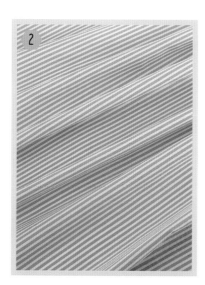

1. Cotton lawn

A crisp, lightweight woven fabric, lawn has a silky feel and is often used for blouses and baby clothes.

2. Poplin

Poplin is a plain weave fabric made from cotton or a cotton/polyester blend. Commonly used in dressmaking, children's clothing and shirts, it's a versatile fabric that has a good drape.

3. Cotton blends

Cotton is sometimes blended with other fibres, such as polyester (to create polycotton), to give the fabric strength and make it easy to care for. Polycotton gives you the best of both worlds: it is affordable, crease-resistant, shrink-resistant and not prone to fading! The mix is usually 65 per cent cotton and 35 per cent polyester, although this can vary. It is a quick-drying, strong fabric, suitable for many types of garments.

4. Crepe

This is a lightweight fabric with a textured surface that is crinkly and slightly rough to touch. Its fluid drape makes it a perfect fabric for loose-fitting dresses and tops.

5. Linen

Linen is a natural fabric made from the fibres of the flax plant. It's a strong, breathable fabric that is known for its cooling properties in warm weather. The downside is how easily it creases, and it can be an expensive buy, but on the plus side you'll have a garment that will last for years!

6. Jersey

As jersey is a knitted fabric, it has stretch, which helps it keep its shape and stay wrinkle-free. It's easy to sew as it doesn't fray, and is comfortable to wear because of its softness... just think of your favourite T-shirt! You may find the fabric curls at the edges when cutting; a good way to prevent this is to use a generous amount of spray starch then press the fabric flat (the starch will wash away).

7. Denim

Indigo denim is woven with one white and one blue thread, causing one side of the fabric to remain blue and the other white, as seen in western-style jeans! But denim can come in many different shades, colours and weights, making it suitable for anything from overalls to blouses. Made from cotton, denim has a characteristic diagonal weave and tends to become softer with wear.

8. Chambray

This is a plain weave fabric that is typically light blue in colour. Although it looks a little like denim, chambray doesn't have the same diagonal weave. It makes a good choice of fabric for shirts and dresses and has a clean, smart look.

9. Corduroy/needlecord

The 'cord' in corduroy is composed of tufted cords, varying in width from fine 'baby' cord to chunky 'jumbo' cord. The finer cords are good for garments that need drape; chunky cords work well for coats and jackets.

10. Velvet

Velvet has a soft pile on the right side and a flat surface on the wrong side. The fibres can range from anything from silk to cotton to wool, although synthetic fibres are now available and are easier to work with as they fray less. Velvet gives a luxurious feel to a garment and is a good fabric to use for jackets and evening wear.

11. Wool

Wool usually comes from the fleece of sheep, although speciality wools are available from goats, llamas and alpacas amongst others. It comes in many grades – the finer grades are suitable for dressmaking and the coarser grades for outerwear, as they are stronger and more durable. Wool has a luxurious feel and makes comfortable clothing.

12. Silk

The best-known silk comes from the larvae of the mulberry silk worm, has a fine texture and reflects the light, giving it a glamorous appearance. I wouldn't recommend sewing with silk for a beginner sewer – it can be slippery to work with, and pins can leave visible holes in the delicate fabric.

UPCYCLING FABRIC

There are many benefits to upcycling fabrics, whether that's from your own wardrobe or from a charity shop/thrift store. You're not just helping the environment and saving money, you'll be working with fabrics that are meant for purpose (if you've ever wondered what the best fabric for a dress is, what better than an actual dress!) and have been pre-washed, so any fading or shrinking has already happened. You can also find some amazing vintage fabrics in charity shops/thrift stores, and look out for unusual fastenings and embellishments. It could be worth buying a blouse simply because you love the buttons, as it will probably be more affordable than buying the actual buttons on their own!

The denim for this gorgeous little dress came from a pair of jeans I found in a charity shop!

- Go into a shop looking at the fabrics not the garments; you may not like the style of that shirt but the fabric may make a fabulous skirt (see page 64). Bear in mind, of course, that the larger the garment, the more fabric you'll have.
- Beware of darts in ladies' shirts – men's shirts don't usually have them, so the fabric is more useable.
- Check each purchase for wear and tear and stains, broken zips and missing buttons, and wash before use.
- For the projects in this book I've chosen the kind of garments you'll easily find in charity shops/thrift stores, but look carefully and you'll find some real gems!

FABRIC TERMINOLOGY

RIGHT/WRONG SIDE

The 'right' side of the fabric is the side you want to see, i.e. the front; the 'wrong' side is the back of the fabric, and is usually paler in printed fabrics. Woven fabrics sometimes have no right or wrong sides, but make sure you use the same sides on all your pattern pieces, as one panel cut with a different side would look really odd!

DIRECTIONAL PRINTS

Some fabrics have a print that only works in one direction (such as the farm print, shown right), so consider this when placing your pattern pieces. A non-directional fabric (such as the diamonds shown far right) can be used upside down as well, which could save quite a lot of fabric with clever pattern placement. Some dressmaking patterns are not suitable for directional prints.

NAP

Fabrics such as fleece, corduroy and velvet have raised fibres which are usually directional. You can feel the nap by running your hand over it: 'with the nap' gives a smooth finish, 'against the nap' gives a slightly rougher finish and a darker shade. If you're following a pattern you'll be advised as to which way to use the fabric – it's important that the nap is running in the same direction for each piece.

HANDLE

This is simply the feel of the fabric as you hold it. It may be firm, rough or smooth, cool or warm, heavy or stretchy.

MERCERIZED

Cotton that has been through a finishing treatment to produce a lustrous, strong finish, sometimes called 'pearle'.

COLOUR FASTNESS

Fabric that retains its colour after washing.

Right and wrong sides of a printed fabric.

Right and wrong sides of a woven fabric.

A directional print.

A non-directional print.

Mercerized cotton.

INTERFACING

Collars, cuffs, necklines, waistbands and pockets invariably require interfacing to give them strength and stability. It can help to prevent the fabric stretching and to give neat edges; jersey garments particularly benefit from interfacing around the neckline to stop them sagging and stretching. Interfacing is available in woven and non-woven types, fusible or sew-in, usually in black or white.

Your pattern will tell you which is best for your garment and it is generally cut to the same size as your pattern piece.

AVAILABLE OPTIONS

⊕ Fusible interfacing has small dots of glue on one side, which adhere the interfacing to fabric when ironed. This is my preferred interfacing, I use the woven variety in a similar weight to my fabric.

⊕ Sew-in interfacing is usually used with fine fabrics like silk, which may wrinkle if a fusible is used, or fabrics embellished with embroidery or sequins that can't be ironed.

⊕ Non-woven interfacings are a little stiffer than woven, making them more suitable for collars and cuffs.

⊕ Woven interfacing behaves very much like fabric, allowing your garment to keep its natural drape. Cut it on the same grain as your fabric.

⊕ Knitted interfacings are softer than woven, and have stretch in all directions. This is useful as it allows the fabric to drape even though it's stabilized; these can be used on woven fabrics.

⊕ Fusible sheer is a perfect lightweight interfacing for silky fabrics.

⊕ Heavy-weight interfacing is used in coats and jackets.

24

Non-woven interfacings.

Woven interfacing.

Knitted interfacing.

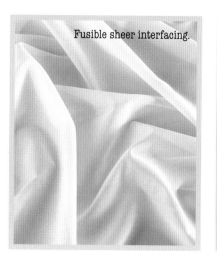
Fusible sheer interfacing.

Heavy-weight interfacing.

THREADS

There are so many threads on the market that it can be hard to know where to start. So here's a little information that may make choosing easier. I always recommend a decent-quality thread, but what makes thread good quality? It's mainly the 'tensile' strength, which helps to lengthen the life of your seams.

Look for a smooth thread. Your thread will be travelling through the eye of your needle at high speed and if a thread is uneven it can weaken and may even twist. In extreme cases, it could even wear out the tension discs on your machine. Inexpensive thread might also shed rough filaments that could build up inside your sewing machine.

It is recommended that you try to use the same fibre content as your fabric – cotton with cotton, polyester with synthetic, etc. – although I don't always follow the rules. There are also different weights of threads to consider. Here are the basics:

⊕ Cotton thread is the most used natural fibre. However, synthetic thread does tend to be stronger and more resistant to colour fading. The best of both worlds is corespun thread, which has a polyester core with cotton fibres wrapped around it.

⊕ Silk thread is very thin so won't make holes in fine fabrics, making it useful for tacking/basting tailored items.

⊕ Topstitching thread is a thick, strong polyester thread used for stitching that can be seen on top of your work (e.g. on jeans) and is perfect for sewing buttonholes.

⊕ Invisible thread (see below) is made from a single filament of either polyester or nylon. This thread is useful for those projects where you want the stitches to be invisible, so is great for hemming both woven and stretch fabrics. Use the thread in the top of the machine with a neutral colour in the bobbin.

⊕ Embroidery thread is usually made from rayon as it's reflective and fine, designed to really show off your decorative stitches.

⊕ Metallic thread is a decorative rayon fibre that can be used in both sewing machines and embroidery machines. You will benefit from investing in a metallic needle (see page 10), which has a smooth coating around the eye to help stop friction from the metallic threads and therefore prevent breakage.

⊕ Thread weights can be confusing but, put simply, a smaller weight number (wt) depicts a heavier thread. As a rough guide, choose a 40wt for dressmaking, and a 50wt or 60wt for appliqué and filling your bobbin. 20–30wt is a thick thread for topstitching and decorative work. If your thread weight looks like a fraction, i.e. 60/2, the first number is the weight and the second is how many strands in the thread. If you're still confused then choose an all-purpose 50wt, which should work with most of your projects.

⊕ My main advice is to avoid threads that look 'fluffy', as this can be a sign of poor quality. Also, invest in as many colours as you can so that you never have to compromise!

DRESSMAKING KNOW-HOW

PRESSING OR IRONING?

Your iron is a crucial dressmaking tool, and you'll need it for both pressing and ironing. But what's the difference?

Pressing is just that: lift the iron on and off the fabric without gliding, which could distort it. Give a blast of steam if you wish. Press pleats, folds, seams and hems. Pressed folds are intended to be permanent, and can even survive a wash. Ironing is simply when the iron passes across the fabric without lifting to take creases away. Use steam if you wish (see top image, right).

It is always wise to test iron a small piece of the fabric you're using to make sure the heat won't make the fabric surface shiny and that you're using the correct temperature. A pressing cloth may help here (see second image from top, right).

When you've sewn your seam, 'meld' it before pressing it open by passing the iron over the stitches – they will embed into the fabric. Then press the seam open.

If your seam is on the edge, for instance with a collar, you should still press the seam open; you'll find you have a neater, sharper edge. A wooden point presser/tailors' board is worth the investment if you're making a lot of shirts – it allows you to press the seam open on a collar whilst the wood absorbs steam and helps to set the seam. The one shown right doubles up as a 'clapper', which is pressed over the seam when hot to set it.

A tailor's ham (see below left) is a sawdust-filled tool that is shaped to go under shoulders, sleeve heads and princess seams to enable you to press without flattening the garment. The sawdust absorbs heat and moisture. A seam roll (see below, centre) works in a similar way but is a longer shape; this is one I made myself.

Using a cardboard tube (see below right) is an effective way of pressing straight seams open without leaving indentations from the seam allowances in the fabric.

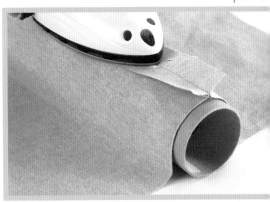

MEASURING YOURSELF

Whether you're making clothes for yourself or someone else, measuring is vitally important to ensure a good fit. Patterns vary in size from one manufacturer to another and won't necessarily match the ready-to-wear dress size you'd choose in a shop, so don't worry if your measurements mean you're making a larger dress size of garment than you'd normally buy!

Measure yourself wearing the underwear you'll wear with your garment. Stand straight in front of a mirror with your feet together. The tape measure should be snug but not tight, and don't leave any fingers under the tape measure. If your weight tends to fluctuate, it's a good idea to re-measure your bust, waist and hips before making a new garment.

It's also easy to measure someone else. If they're not comfortable wearing their underwear, ask them to pop on something snug that won't add anything extra to the measurements.

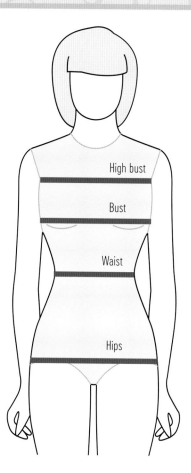

TAKING KEY MEASUREMENTS

High bust
Measure around the body above the bust, just under the arms; this will be approximately 7.5cm (3in) below the neck.

Bust
Take the tape measure around your body at the fullest part of the bust, keeping it straight and flat.

Waist
The waist is generally just above the belly button, at the narrowest part of the body. An easy way to find your waist is to tie a piece of elastic around your middle – it should roll by itself to the smallest part of your waist. Measure and take note, then leave the elastic in place as it will help when we come to the vertical measurements.

Hips
Take the measure around the fullest part of your hips; this is often a standard measurement of 20cm (8in) larger than the waist measurement, but will vary from person to person.

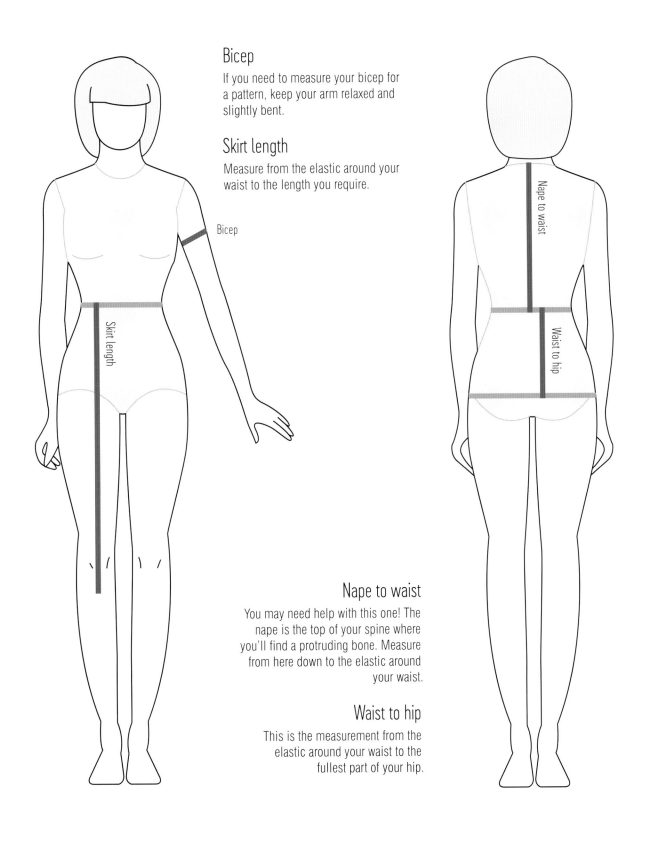

Bicep

If you need to measure your bicep for a pattern, keep your arm relaxed and slightly bent.

Skirt length

Measure from the elastic around your waist to the length you require.

Bicep

Skirt length

Nape to waist

Waist to hip

Nape to waist

You may need help with this one! The nape is the top of your spine where you'll find a protruding bone. Measure from here down to the elastic around your waist.

Waist to hip

This is the measurement from the elastic around your waist to the fullest part of your hip.

Dress length

Measure from the nape of the neck to the length you require.

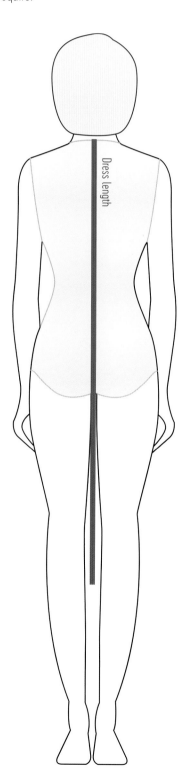

Dress length

MEASUREMENT CONSIDERATIONS

⊕ Traditional patterns are made to fit a B cup bust; if you're not this size, you may have to make a bust adjustment to your pattern. This is how to work out your cup size: take your full bust measurement and subtract your high bust measurement. If the difference is 2.5cm (1in) you're an A cup, 5cm (2in) is a B cup, 7.5cm (3in) is a C cup, 10cm (4in) is a D cup and so on.

⊕ The sleeve measurement is taken from the shoulder; with your arm slightly bent, measure along the arm to the wrist.

⊕ If you're making men's attire, the measurements are similar except that the full bust measurement is instead a chest measurement. You may also need to take a neck measurement: this is the circumference of the neck around the Adam's apple, usually 5cm (2in) above the collar bone.

⊕ Baby patterns just ask for length and weight.

⊕ For toddlers you'll need just chest, waist and height; patterns usually allow space for nappies/diapers.

⊕ For a child you'll need chest, waist, hips, back/waist length and height measurements.

⊕ If you're buying patterns from a store, do look in the back of the catalogues and you'll find lots of useful information about measuring that related to the patterns inside.

Ease

Ease is the difference between the measurements of your body and the finished garment. A garment without ease would be literally skin tight – fine if you're making a bodycon-style fitted stretch dress, but if you used a woven fabric you'd have difficulty moving!

Take a look on the back of a commercial dress pattern and you'll probably see that the finished measurements are slightly larger than yours. As a general guideline, if you're making a garment using your measurements without a pattern, add a couple of inches to the bust, waist and hips, then any extra adjustments can be made once you've made a toile. Depending on the style of your garment, you may want it to be tighter or looser.

CHOOSING A PATTERN

When you're first starting out on your dressmaking journey, I'd suggest you choose a garment that is quite similar to your usual style so you know it will suit you. There would be nothing worse than spending hours making a dress only to realize when you put it on that it's just not for you!

⊕ Many manufacturers have an 'easy' range of patterns designed with the beginner in mind, with simple-to-follow instructions and basic sewing techniques.
⊕ Children's patterns are a good place to start, as the garments rarely have darts and use simple closures.
⊕ Patterns that cover more than one garment offer great value for money.
⊕ Don't take too much notice of the colours and prints of the garments on the packet – just look at the style, as you can choose any colour you like!
⊕ Most dress patterns cover several sizes, which is a bonus for those of us whose top isn't the same size as our bottom, as you can grade the pattern across the sizes. Some manufacturers will split the sizes across two packets. If you find you are in between the packet sizes, go for the measurement that matches your upper bust. It's a lot easier to adjust the cup, waist and hip size than to tackle the shoulders and neckline! Sizing information will be on the back of the envelope so you can see before buying.

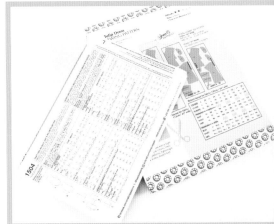

Read the information on the back of your pattern before buying fabric. This will inform you of the type and amount of fabric needed, plus any notions such as zips and fasteners required.

If you're using stretch fabric there may be a guide as to how stretchy the fabric needs to be for the garment you've chosen. Hold your fabric over the short line unstretched, then stretch to the longer line to test stretchability!

UNDERSTANDING PATTERN SYMBOLS

Fitting pattern pieces together is a bit like constructing a jigsaw, with notches and markings to help fit the pieces together perfectly. Information about your pattern symbols will be in the pattern envelope, along with an explanation of abbreviations used. Symbols will vary from one manufacturer to another, but here's a general overview of the most commonly used ones.

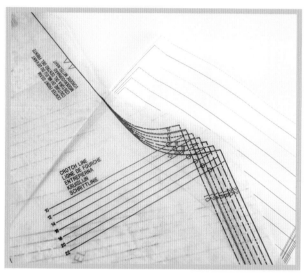

Multi-sized patterns will have the outline of each size marked in dashes and dots or coloured lines. It's important to stick to the correct line when cutting out your size, so it may help to highlight your size with a coloured pen (as shown above).

Each pattern piece will have the number or name, plus the amount of pieces that need to be cut.

The long line, sometimes with an arrow at one or both ends, is the grainline. This shows how the pattern needs to be placed on the fabric. Unless you are cutting on the bias, the grainline will be parallel to the fabric's selvedge/selvage. If the pattern isn't cut straight on the grain it may not hang well.

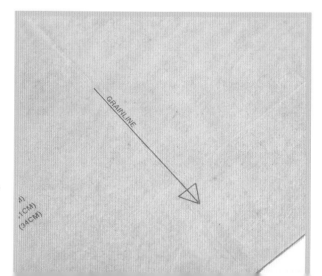

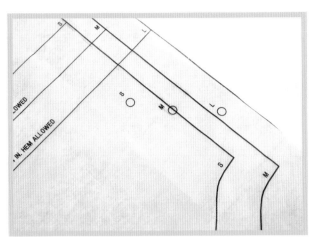

Dots can mark the position of the end of a zip, dart or vent, or indicate pocket placement, for example, so make sure you follow the pattern instructions for an explanation.

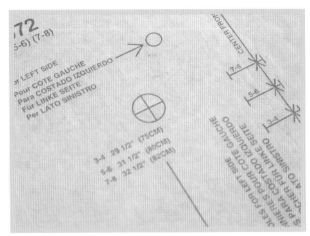

A circle with a cross inside it marks the apex, the fullest part, of the bust, hip or shoulder.

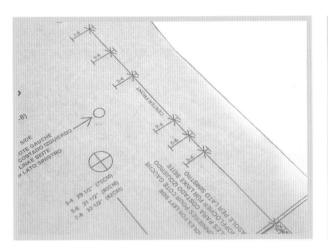

The symbol for a buttonhole is generally a straight line with a bar at each end. Make sure you mark the ones for your size.

Darts are depicted by long 'V' shapes with either single or double points (see more on page 43).

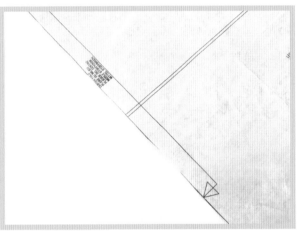

Fold arrows indicate that the pattern edge needs to be placed on folded fabric so that when opened out, the fabric piece is double the width of the pattern, and symmetrical.

If your garment needs to be lengthened or shortened, don't be tempted to simply take up the hem. There will be a line indicating the best area for alteration.

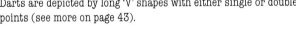

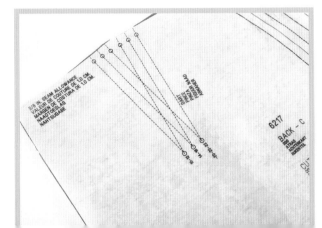

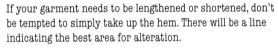

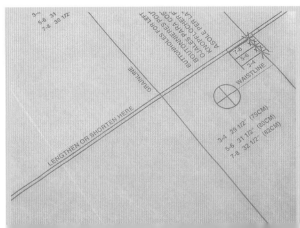

CUTTING OUT YOUR PATTERN

Read the instructions before cutting your pattern – you'll find valuable information about markings, terminology and pattern placement. Make a note of the pattern pieces you need to use for the garment you're making; mark the actual pattern pieces if that makes it easier.

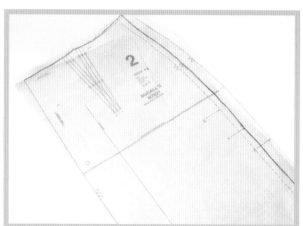

1 Roughly cut around the pieces you need, then iron them! You won't have accurate sizing if there are any creases in the paper.

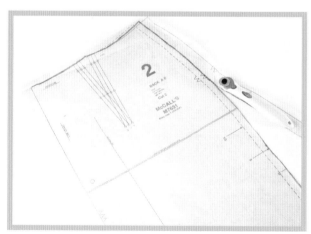

2 You may find it helpful to draw around the pattern size you need with a coloured pen. If your measurements cross over two or three sizes, use your French curve to draw in smooth lines that bridge the gap between the larger and the smaller sizes.

3 Cut your pattern carefully with sharp scissors or a rotary cutter. A small cutter, 28mm in size, will give you the best accuracy. Practise first, as you'll need a steady hand!

PATTERN MATCHING

My honest pattern-matching advice for a beginner sewer is: don't pattern match! Instead, choose a fabric with a small pattern that won't need matching, and avoid checks and horizontal stripes until you're confident in matching prints. But when you are ready to give it a go, here is all you need to know.

⊕ Start by reading your pattern first, as some will state that they're not suitable for pattern matching.

⊕ You will need to buy extra fabric when pattern matching, and the amount will depend on the pattern repeat on the fabric itself.

⊕ Consider the placement of the pattern on your fabric – avoid placing very noticeable parts of the print over the apex of the garment. For instance, putting a large flower over the bust may not give the most flattering result!

⊕ You'll rarely have a perfect pattern match in every seam of your garment, so match the areas that are most noticeable. For instance, the front of a sleeve is seen more than the shoulders, so choose that point to start matching. The centre back will be more noticeable than the side seams, so make that your starting point.

⊕ Bear in mind that your pattern must match at the stitched seam, not the seam allowance, so it may help to mark the seam allowance on your pattern.

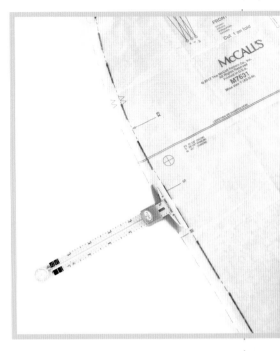

Draw on your seam allowance so that you know precisely where your stitched seams will sit.

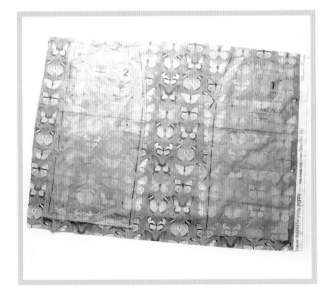

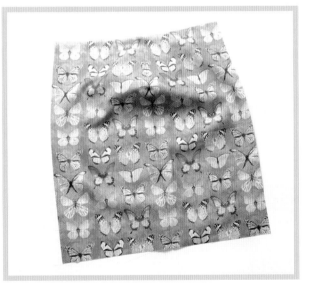

1 Pin two pattern pieces that you need to match side by side on your fabric. Look for a matching point – I've chosen the centre of these butterflies along the straight part of the side seams; you can see the wastage in the centre of the two patterns. I will match the most visible area, from the hem to the hip.

2 Cut out your pieces and pin them right sides together; pinning along the stitch line may help when sewing. Turn your work over to make sure the pattern matches perfectly. Sew the seam, removing the pins as you go.

TRANSFERRING PATTERN SYMBOLS

Here are a few ways to transfer your pattern marks accurately onto your fabric. Bear in mind that the pattern pieces will include a 1.5cm (⁵⁄₈in) seam allowance unless otherwise stated.

NOTCHES

Triangular notches at the sides of the pattern will help you to line up the seams. Some people prefer to mirror the triangles when cutting out, whereas others prefer to snip into the triangle with a sharp pair of scissors – this won't weaken the seam if the snips are kept small. Make sure to match single triangles with single and double with double; single are usually at the front of the garment and double at the back.

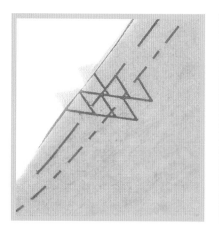 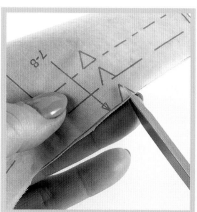

DOTS

Dots (see page 33) can be marked with erasable ink or chalk pens. Push a pin through the dot and both layers of fabric, then lift the pattern off the fabric with the pin still in place and mark the entry point of the pin on the wrong sides of the fabric.

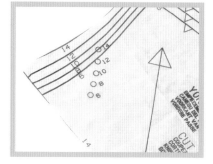 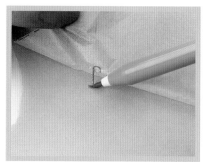

TRACING WHEEL

I find a quick way of transferring any markings is to use a tracing wheel and carbon paper. Have your fabric pieces facing each other right sides together with your pattern pinned on top. Place the carbon paper, ink side up, underneath the fabric.

Press quite hard on the wheel and slowly run it over your markings. Most of your marks will be within the seam allowance, but the ink will wash out so don't worry if it's seen. Carefully unpin the pattern without disturbing the fabric, turn the fabric over and re-pin the pattern – it will be facing down. Re-trace the markings.

TAILOR'S TACKS

These are a traditional way of marking patterns.

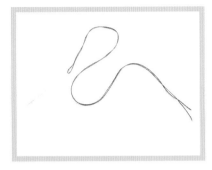

1 Run a length of thread through your needle, so that both strands are the same length (there is no need to tie a knot in the end). This is an opportunity to use that bargain thread that turned out to be too weak to sew with!

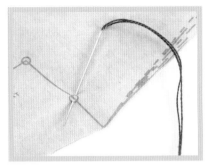

2 Take the needle through one side of the dot on the tissue pattern, and straight through the fabric, whether that's one or two layers. Bring the needle up on the opposite side of the dot.

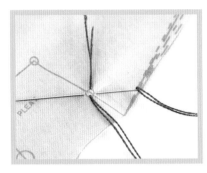

3 Pull the needle through leaving about 2.5cm (1in) of tail thread, then re-insert the needle at right angles to your first stitch.

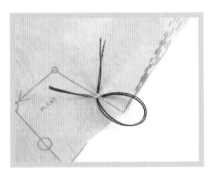

4 Trim off the thread, leaving a loop and two 2.5cm (1in) tail threads.

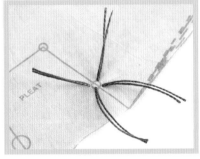

5 Snip through the loop to make four 'tufts'.

6 Sew as many tacks as your pattern requires, then carefully peel back the tissue pattern.

7 Your thread markings will be left behind in your fabric – don't forget to remove them once you've finished sewing!

8 If you're sewing through two layers of fabric, part the fabric carefully without pulling the threads through. Snip the threads in between the two layers.

9 You'll now have even markings on both sides of the fabric.

CUTTING FABRIC

It's important to understand how to position your patterns on fabric before cutting, so here are some helpful tips.

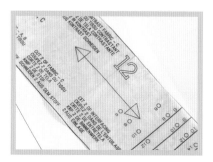

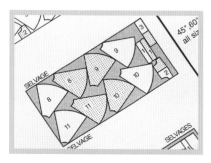

38

Check your pattern's grainline to see how it needs to be placed on your fabric: you'll see a line or arrow that needs to be placed parallel to the selvedge/selvage (see also page 32).

If the grainline line or arrow is at an angle across the pattern this means the fabric will be cut on the bias (at a 45-degree angle), giving it more stretch and drape; when you place the arrow parallel to the selvedge/selvage, the pattern piece will sit diagonally across the fabric.

Your instructions will usually give diagrams of pattern placement to make the best use of fabric depending on the fabric width, and also the best way to fold it to reduce wastage. Remember, with non-directional prints and plain fabrics, some of your pieces can be cut upside down – this can save a lot of fabric!

If your pattern says to 'cut two' then these pieces are mirror-imaged; cut two pieces at once with the right sides of the fabric facing.

To pre-wash or not?

For dressmaking I do, as even though most modern fabrics don't need to be pre-washed, I'd rather see how the fabric behaves when washed before I spend a day making a garment. Look for shrinkage and colour fastness, and bear in mind that fabric sometimes has a different feel (handle) after washing. It's also useful to know how the fabric will dry and how much ironing it will need before it is made into a garment!

Using pattern weights

Pattern weights are just as the name describes: weighted objects that you place around the edges of your pattern when it is on top of your fabric, to hold it in place while you cut. They remove the need to use pins, which can sometimes cause the fabric to pucker or stretch slightly as you insert them. Pattern weights are very quick to use... simply pop them on top and off you go! You don't need to spend a lot of money on them – a handful of clean pebbles will do, or you could make your own, like the ones shown here, which are each made from just two squares of fabric and a handful of rice.

MAKING A TOILE

A toile (also known as a calico or muslin) is a sample garment, depending on where in the world you live! Making a toile may seem like a time-consuming exercise, but in the long run it may save you time and money. By constructing the garment in affordable fabric first, you can check both the fit and style before committing to your chosen fabric. As a toile is mainly for fit, it's not necessary to add extras like pockets or linings. Use a cheap woven fabric such as calico/muslin for your toile, unless you're making a stretch garment, in which case choose a similar stretch fabric. For looser fitting clothes it may not be necessary to make a toile, but for anything that is closely fitted I would recommend it.

⊕ Cut out your pattern pieces from calico and transfer any markings. Label each section by writing on it, and transfer any apex markings. Draw a line straight down the centre front and centre back, and mark across the hip line of a skirt. These lines will help with the alignment of the pieces when sewn together.

⊕ Sew the calico pieces together as your pattern instructs, starting with the darts. Use a long stitch as you may need to unpick them! Finish by pressing.

⊕ Try on your toile (or fit it to a dress form if you have one) and assess the fit. Does the waistline sit on your waistline? Is the apex of the bust sitting over the fullest part of your bust? Are the lines you've drawn down the front of the pattern sitting straight down your body, and do the shoulder seams sit straight across your shoulders? Note any tightness or gaping so you can adjust these issues on the pattern.

⊕ Some changes are simple, like lowering a neckline or adjusting the length; sometimes increasing or decreasing the seam allowance may be all the adjustment you need. Most patterns are graded in sizes so, for instance, if your hips measure one size and your waist a different size, draw a line from one size to another on the pattern to create the right sized pattern for you.

⊕ I felt the darts on my shirt toile were a little low and would benefit from pointing towards the bust apex. I re-drew on my toile where I wanted the darts to point, transferred the markings to my pattern then sewed the new darts in place. A much better fit!

⊕ Adjusting the bust on a pattern is a bit more involved but worth the time taken to create the perfect fit. If your toile is tight across the bust but fits on the shoulders, a full bust adjustment is required. If the shoulders fit but the bust is loose, then a small bust adjustment is needed.

MACHINE STITCHES

Depending on your machine, you may have two or two hundred stitches – utility stitches for project construction and decorative stitches for embellishment. Take a look in the manufacturer's manual to see the recommended presser feet to use with the different stitches. In many cases the feet are lettered and some machines will display the foot required on the screen. Here you'll find the stitches I use most for dressmaking.

STRAIGHT STITCH

The most useful stitch on your machine! Use for joining fabric, gathering, topstitching and tacking/basting. You should be able to alter the length of the stitch where necessary on your machine. On many machines, the stitch width function will swing the needle from left to right. By contrast, adjusting the length of the stitch doesn't affect the needle: it changes the rate at which the feed dogs draw the fabric through. A shorter stitch forms a strong seam and is preferable to use with fine fabrics. The majority of sewing machines will default to a 2.4 or 2.5mm stitch length – this is suitable for most fabrics. Long stitches are sewn with a looser tension and are easy to remove, making them an appropriate choice for tacking/basting. You may prefer to use a longer stitch when topstitching.

TRIPLE STRAIGHT STITCH

This is a stitch designed for stretch fabrics, as the backstitch technique has a little 'give', preventing the stitches from breaking when stretched. It also creates a thick line of stitching, which makes a useful topstitch on fabrics like denim.

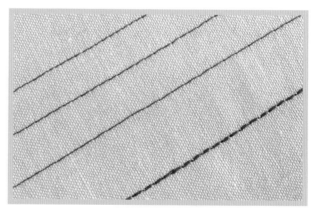

GATHERING

Although you can buy a gathering foot for your sewing machine, you can also create a tight and accurate gather just by machine stitching. Use a long stitch and loosen your tension slightly, then sew two rows of stitches about 5mm (¼in) apart. This will help the gathered seam to sit flat. Leave long threads at each end, then gently pull the bottom threads to gather the fabric.

Above: short 1.5mm straight stitch is shown at the top, then standard 2.5mm straight stitch, then 5mm tacking/basting stitch, and at the bottom is triple straight stitch.

Below: triple straight stitch topstitching on denim.

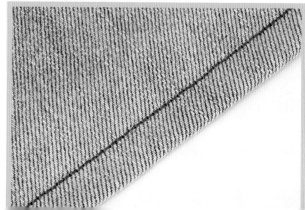

ZIGZAG STITCH

This versatile stitch has many uses. If you don't have decorative stitches on your machine, try using your zigzag stitch to create a pretty border. It's also good for over-edge stitching to finish seams – sew right up to the edge of your fabric and use a small length of stitch if you have the capability. It's also a useful stretch stitch for sewing in elastic, and a very narrow zigzag stitch can be used for seams on stretch fabric.

BLIND-HEM STITCH

This stitch sews along the inside of your hem with a straight stitch, then occasionally throws a zigzag stitch into the fold of the hem, catching just a couple of threads to keep the stitches as invisible as possible from the right side of your project. Although used mainly around hems, this is also a useful stitch for adding appliqué (see page 81). A blind-hem stitch foot can be used (see page 17), which has an adjustable guide.

BUTTONHOLE STITCH

A buttonhole stitch is a short zigzag stitch, sewn using a special presser foot on your machine (see page 16). You can choose assorted styles of hole depending on your project and your machine. I use a standard box buttonhole for shirts, blouses, skirts and trousers, and a rounded buttonhole for fine fabrics. A keyhole works well with heavy fabrics and buttons with shanks, making it perfect for coats and jackets. A buttonhole with a zigzag edge is good for stretch fabrics.

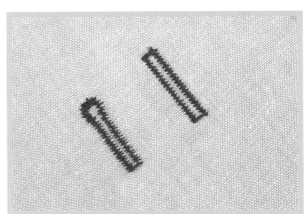

DECORATIVE STITCHES

Many machines will have a selection of decorative stitches that can be used around hems, pockets, cuffs and collars to add interest and a little fun to plain or softly patterned fabrics.

SPECIAL STITCHES

You might already be familiar with these dressmaking stitches as they are crucial to help make your garments look well-made.

STAY STITCH

This is a row of stitches sewn to a single layer of fabric to help stabilize it and prevent stretching around curved areas such as necklines and armholes. This is an important technique, particularly for stretch fabrics to make sure they keep their shape. Woven fabric becomes slightly stretchy when cut on the bias and when a curved shape is cut; sew inside the seam allowance so that the stitches aren't seen on the garment. There is no need to remove the stitches.

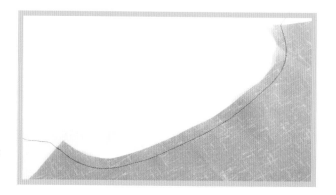

UNDERSTITCHING

42

Understitching is the method of sewing the facing of a garment to the seam allowance, usually around the neckline. This helps to prevent the facing from rolling to the outside, and isn't visible on the finished garment.

EASE STITCHING

1 This stitch is used to tighten fabric without gathering, most commonly in fitted sleeves. Your pattern will have two points in the seam allowance at the top of the sleeve, marked here in green.

2 Transfer these marks to your fabric then sew between the two marks slightly within the seam allowance. It may help to mark the seam allowance so you have an accurate guide.

3 Pull the thread as if you were gathering, but make sure the stitches don't pucker the fabric. It is possible to 'shrink' the stitch line considerably without any gathers!

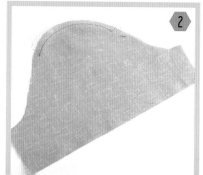
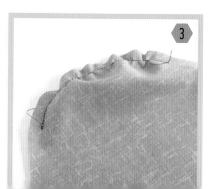

DARTS

Darts give a garment three-dimensional shape; they may seem daunting, but really you just pinch the fabric and sew it, forcing the fabric into a new shape. You may see single-ended darts in bodices and waistbands, or double-ended darts in dresses. Some garments will have both.

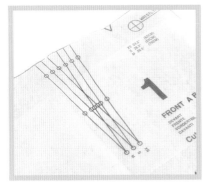

Single-ended dart.

1 Transfer the dart markings accurately to the wrong side of your fabric (see pages 36–37).

2 Fold the dart in half, right sides together, with the markings matching. Sew along the dart line; always sew from the edge of the fabric towards the centre.

3 When you come to the end of the dart, sew a couple of stitches along the fold, and leave the threads long before cutting. Tie the two threads together and knot to stop the stitches coming undone. Never backstitch at the end of a dart, as it may make the seam a bit bulky (3a). It's the same process for a double-ended dart; this time start sewing from the centre of the dart (3b). The threads can either be trimmed or hand-sewn into the dart.

4 Press the dart. Bust darts are pressed downwards; generally waist darts are pressed towards the side seams.

Double-ended dart.

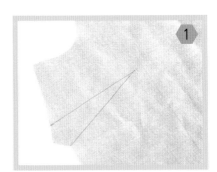

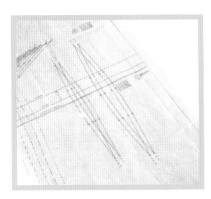

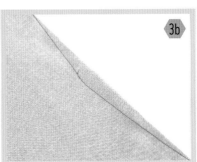

SEAMS

SEAM ALLOWANCE

This is the distance from the raw edge of your fabric to the line of stitches. Read the instructions or pattern for your project as the seam allowance will vary; dressmakers generally use 1.5cm (⅝in). However, I recently started making up a man's shirt without reading the instructions and automatically used a 1.5cm (⅝in) seam allowance. I was halfway through the collar before I realized it should have been 5mm (¼in)... I now need to find a small boy for that shirt to fit!

For most of your seams, use the default straight stitch length on your computerized sewing machine, which is usually 2.5 (this is mm); on mechanical machines you'll need to turn a knob to choose the right setting. A shorter stitch may work well on finer fabric, but use a long stitch for tacking/basting or gathering. For decorative topstitching the choice is yours. Test on a scrap piece of fabric first to make sure you're happy with the finished effect.

Altering the stitch length doesn't change the needle action, but the speed at which the feed dogs draw the fabric under the needle.

Read your pattern instructions to see if the designer recommends pressing the finished seams open or to one side.

FINISHING SEAMS

I don't worry too much about finishing seams that won't be seen, for instance inside lined bags, but for dressmaking, neat, unfrayed edges give a more professional look. How you finish your seams is a matter of choice.

⊕ Use **pinking shears** to trim the raw edges for a quick way to stop fabric from fraying.

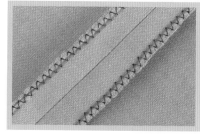

⊕ As a good alternative to pinking shears, use a **zigzag stitch**.

⊕ To create a **clean edge finish** on your seam, neaten the raw edges by folding over once or twice and hemming. This is quite time-consuming and may create too much bulk on finer fabrics.

⊕ An **overlocker/serger** gives a really professional-looking finish. These machines take the threads over the edge of the fabric, trimming the edge with a blade as you sew. However, if you don't want to go to the extra expense, many sewing machines will have an **over-edge stitch** that does a similar job.

FRENCH SEAMS

This seam requires no finishing, as the raw edges can't be seen – the seam looks equally neat on both the inside and outside of your work. Use this on fine or sheer fabrics or where a raw seam could look ugly. Use the same colour thread as your fabric.

1 Sew your fabrics wrong sides together, taking a 1cm (³⁄₈in) seam allowance. Trim the seam allowance back to 3mm (¹⁄₈in).

2 Fold the fabric over the seam, right sides together. Sew with a 5mm (¹⁄₄in) seam allowance, trapping the raw edges in the centre. Open out and press.

3 The result is a neat seam with no raw edges showing from either side.

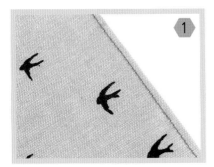
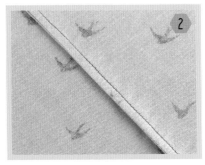

FLAT-FELLED SEAMS

A flat-felled seam is used to strengthen the seams on garments that tend to take a bit of stress, like the inside leg seam of jeans, or childrenswear. It makes a neat join, with no raw edges showing on either side of the garment. This seam can be sewn from either side of the fabric, but the most common way is to sew the fabric from the right side. Use either the same colour or a contrasting thread.

1 Sew a 1.5cm (⅝in) seam allowance with your fabric wrong sides together. Press the seam open. Trim away one seam allowance, taking it to 5mm (¼in).

2 Fold the wider seam allowance over the narrow one and press.

3 Tuck the raw edge of the wider seam allowance under and press again, making sure the flap of fabric is the same width all the way along. Topstitch close to the fold, trapping the raw edges inside the seam.

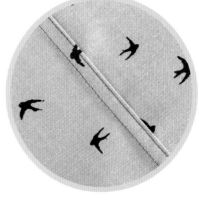

Flat-felled seam viewed from the right side.

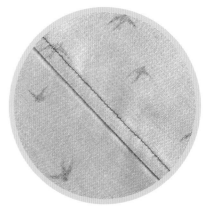

Flat-felled seam viewed from the wrong side.

HEMS

Hems neaten the raw edges of your fabric. Fabrics that don't fray, such as felt, don't need to be hemmed. For woven fabrics I'd suggest folding the edge over twice for a neat finish.

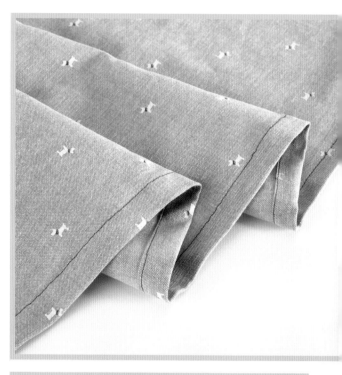

TOPSTITCHED HEM

This is the simplest hem to make: measure and mark the length of hem and pin. Press the hem to the wrong side, removing the pins as you go. Open out the hem and fold the raw edge under; press again. Re-fold the original hemline so that the raw edge is trapped inside the fold. Topstitch on your machine.

MACHINE-ROLLED HEM

Use a rolled-hem foot on your sewing machine (see page 17), which feeds the raw edge of the fabric through the foot and curls it over to create a very narrow hem. This technique is favoured on fine or lightweight fabrics.

FACED HEM

Whether faced with binding or a deep length of fabric, this is a heavy hem that is suitable for curved hems or where weight is beneficial to garments, such as for wedding dresses. For a deep facing, cut the fabric to the same shape as the hem and sew right sides together. You'll need to finish the raw edge of the facing.

46

BOUND HEM

As with a faced hem, bias binding adds weight to a garment's hem, and can also add a contrasting trim to unlined jackets and circular hems.

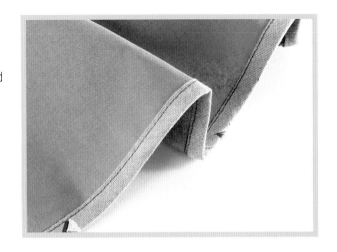

OVERLOCKED/SERGED ROLLED HEM

It's possible to create a tiny rolled hem on your overlocker/ serger which is barely visible, and a good choice for curved hemlines (top image below). Try using with stretch fabrics such as jersey to create a pretty fluted hem on garments like pyjamas and children's clothing (bottom image below).

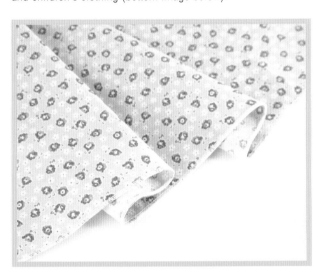

This lovely kimono jacket (made on pages 48–49) uses a rolled hem so as not to overwhelm the delicate, floaty fabric.

Project
KIMONO JACKET

Tip

When sewing fine fabrics, use a walking foot to stop slippage, and a small stitch. Support the garment to the left of the needle to stop the weight distorting the stitch line.

48

Techniques

⊕ Drafting a pattern
⊕ Creating a rolled hem

Notes

Use a 1.5cm ($^5/_8$in) seam allowance

You will need

⊕ Large sheet of drafting or tracing paper, ruler, pencil and French curve
⊕ Fabric: use your body measurements and step 1 to calculate your fabric requirements; my centre back is 81.5cm (32in) and the sleeve is 61cm (24in). I used 2m (2¼yd) of fabric measuring 137cm (54in) wide
⊕ Walking foot (optional)

Measure

⊕ Measure from the nape of your neck to the length of sleeve, then from the nape of your neck to the length. Add 10cm (4in) or so to each measurement, as this is a really easy project to make smaller if you need to.

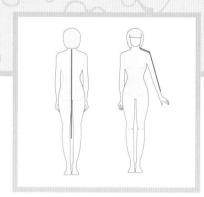

This made-to-measure loose-fitting jacket is simple to make and flattering to wear; choose a floaty fabric to create a beautiful drape. I've used a viscose crepe, which is lightweight and comfortable.

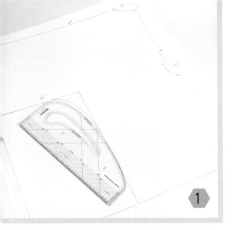

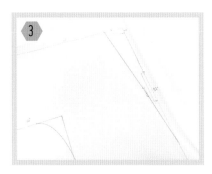

Rolled hem.

1 We'll start by making a pattern on paper. Draw a line for the centre back (mine is 81.5cm/32in plus 10cm/4in) – but draw it down the right-hand side of the paper – you will use this pattern on the fold of the fabric, so we only need to draw out one half of the shape. Draw another line at right angles to the top, to the length of your sleeve measurement plus 10cm (4in): mine is 61cm (24in) plus 10cm (4in), which equals 71cm (28in). Draw in lines along the left-hand side and bottom to complete the rectangle. Measure 33cm (13in) down from the top left-hand corner to form a sleeve, then 36cm (14in) in towards the centre. Join this line to the bottom of the rectangle. You'll see the shape of half of the kimono. Curve a line under the arm, using your French curve. Finally, measure 10cm (4in) to the left from the centre top, and 4cm (1½in) down from the centre top, and draw a curved line for the neck.

2 Cut out your back pattern. Fold your fabric in half and pin your pattern over the top, with the centre back on the fold of the fabric. Cut out your fabric.

3 Go back to your pattern; draw a line from the edge of the neck, tapering it down along the centre back. This new shape will form the front of the jacket.

4 Fold your remaining fabric in half and pin your pattern over the top – don't place the edge on the fold this time as we are creating two separate pieces. Cut out your two front pieces.

5 Sew the front and back pieces right sides together along the shoulders, underarm and side seams – I've used my overlocker/serger for speed, but if you're using a sewing machine, use a 1.5cm (⅝in) seam allowance and finish the seams to stop them fraying.

6 Try your jacket on. Do the sleeves need taking up? Are you happy with the length? At this point you can alter the length and take in the sides if necessary. Finally, hem all around the edges, including the sleeves. A rolled hem creates a pretty effect, either on your machine or overlocker/serger (see page 47).

BINDINGS

Bias binding is a strip of woven fabric that has been cut at a 45-degree angle, which gives it a little stretch. The long edges of the strip are folded to the centre, then the strip can be used to bind around armholes and hems. You may also see it used as a decorative element on pockets. The beauty of it having a slight stretch means it can make a neat, accurate curved hem on garments such as full skirts.

You can buy pre-made bias binding or make your own. The benefit of making your own is that you know you'll have the perfect fabric match! You'll find it helpful to invest in a rotary cutter, ruler, mat and a variety of bias binding makers in different sizes.

Using bias-cut strips is essential for binding curved areas such as armholes and collars.

A rotary cutter, ruler, mat and bias binding maker will make creating your own binding quick and easy.

MAKING BIAS BINDING

1 Cut across your fabric at a 45-degree angle.

2 From this cut, use the edge of your ruler to measure the width of tape you need. The strip needs to be twice the width of the finished bias tape, i.e. for 2.5cm (1in) wide bias binding, cut 5cm (2in) wide strips.

3 To join the strips, place the pieces right sides together at right angles and overlap them slightly. Sew from corner to corner across the two strips, as shown.

4 Trim the seam to about 3mm ($\frac{1}{8}$in). Push one end of the strip through the tape maker and pull – you'll see the sides automatically fold to the centre; press as the tape comes through.

5 Depending on the style of your garment, you can use the binding as a decorative trim (5a), or fold it to the inside to create a clean hem (5b). (See hems on pages 46–47.)

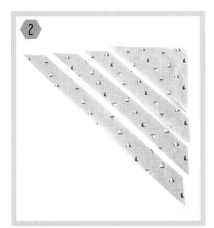

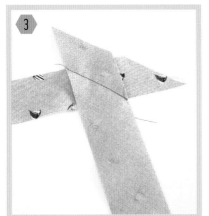

CLOSURES

Usually needed for garments made from woven fabrics that have little stretch, closures come in a variety of choices from buttons to zips and hook-and-loop fastenings to ribbon ties. Some closures are barely seen, such as hooks and eyes or concealed zips, while others can make a fun statement: bold buttons on a plain blouse or brightly coloured snap fasteners on a jacket can really transform an outfit!

HOOKS AND EYES

Hooks and eyes or hooks and bars are usually found at the tops of zips on dresses, or in the waistband of trousers, to help keep a garment secure. Made from metal, they are available mainly in black or silver and in many different sizes, depending on their intended use.

SNAP FASTENERS

Snap fasteners (also known as press studs and poppers) can be plastic or metal and come in many sizes. You'll use them to fasten necklines of sweaters or for baby clothes. Some will need a special tool for fitting, and you'll need to refer to the manufacturer's instructions for use.

BUTTONS

You'll find buttons really useful, not just for closures but also to add decorative elements to your garments.

1 Some buttons have two holes.

2 Some have four.

3 Some are purely decorative – their shapes make them impractical to use with buttonholes.

4 Some buttons have shanks, which makes them more suitable for thick fabrics and knitwear, with no visible holes from the top.

5 To create a shank for a button with holes, sew the button onto the fabric with a cocktail stick or the like underneath. Remove the stick while the needle is still threaded, then wrap the thread around the loose stitches underneath the button before knotting.

6 Create your own decorative buttons by sewing two together.

7 Try tying the thread on top of the button, or wrapping the thread around the edge of the button for a fun effect.

8 To create a perfectly matched button, kits are available to cover buttons in the fabric of your choice. See manufacturer's instructions for how to cover.

53

Buttonhole essentials

Machine-sewn buttonholes are quick and simple to sew; their neat, uniform look makes a row of buttonholes look really smart. Some machines use a four-step process and some just one step. Use stabilizer behind the buttonhole as you sew to help stop the stitches from puckering; I like to use a tear-away stabilizer that I can simply rip away after use. Always test on spare fabric first to make sure you're happy with the size and design of the buttonhole. This will also ensure you are aware of exactly where the machine will start and stop sewing, which is important if you need to line up a row of holes.

Four-step buttonholes require you to stop manually at the length you need, bar tack across the top, then come down the next side and bar tack across the bottom.

A one-step buttonhole makes all the stitches before stopping automatically. The buttonhole foot also measures the size of your button to make the hole a perfect fit!

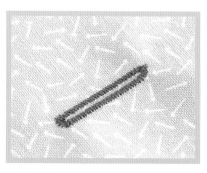

Buttonholes can be shaped or rounded. Round-ended buttonholes are generally used on blouses and fine fabrics as they have a delicate look.

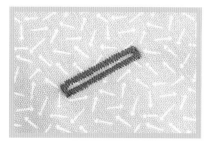

A square buttonhole is best for medium-weight fabrics – you'll see these on shirts and skirts.

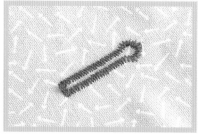

A keyhole buttonhole will accommodate buttons with shanks, or those used on heavy fabrics and garments such as coats and jackets.

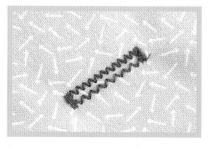

Some machines have a stitch especially for stretch fabric.

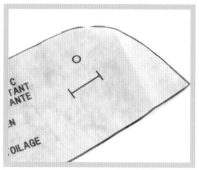

Buttonhole marking on a pattern.

Make sure you transfer the markings accurately to your garment before sewing. Most machines will make their first row of stitches backwards, so place your presser foot over the front end of the marking before sewing.

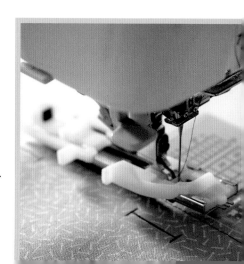

ZIPS

Here are some of the zips I use most frequently:

Continuous zipping

This is bought in lengths; sometimes the sliders are already attached, sometimes you need to attach them yourself. Extra sliders are usually available.

Nylon zips

The most common type of zip and the one I use most often. The coil is a continuous chain as opposed to 'teeth' – if pulled, you'd have one long piece of nylon wire! I choose a zip that is longer than I need, which means I can sew with the slider out of the way, and it can be cut to size so I don't have to worry about buying the exact length of zip I need.

Nylon zips with transparent tape

Perfect for lightweight fabric or for a fabric colour that's difficult to match.

Metal-tooth zips

These are strong zips that are good for outerwear and jeans. They have individual metal teeth that are fixed evenly along the tape.

Open-ended zips

Metal or plastic teeth are fixed along the zip tape. The two sides of the zip come apart completely, making the zip perfect for coats and jackets.

Invisible zips

The zip shouldn't be seen when fitted, apart from the teardrop-shaped zip pull.

Invisible zip closed.

Zip open.

Parts of a zip

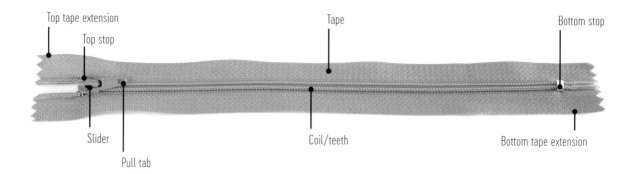

Top tape extension

Top stop

Tape

Bottom stop

Slider

Pull tab

Coil/teeth

Bottom tape extension

Zip tips

⊕ To lubricate a zip and help it run smoothly, try rubbing lip balm, candle wax, soap or a graphite pencil over the teeth. Wipe off any residue.

⊕ Pin the zip in place, then hand tack/baste and remove the pins before sewing. Alternatively, you may find it easier to use a temporary glue instead of tacking/basting your zip by hand, or a fusible quilter's tape may help. Use whichever method you prefer – the important thing is that it enables you to sew a precise line without manoeuvring around pins, and it helps to keep the zip coil centred.

⊕ When approaching the slider as you're sewing in a zip, leave the needle in the down position and manoeuvre the slider out of the way. This will help to keep your stitch line straight.

If you prefer not to tack/baste, a speedy solution is to use a temporary glue before sewing.

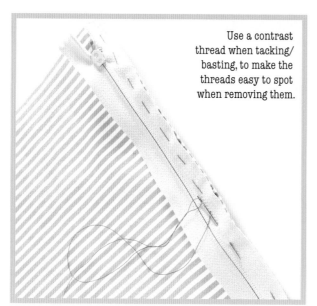

Use a contrast thread when tacking/basting, to make the threads easy to spot when removing them.

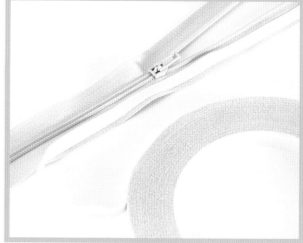

Fusible quilter's tape is another time-saving option.

Inserting a concealed zip

The only part of a concealed zip that should be visible is the zip pull, making it a perfect closure for a dress or skirt where you'd like to keep the seam line clean.

A concealed zip doesn't show the coil from the top and usually has a tear drop-shaped pull; it is sewn into the garment prior to the seam being sewn.

A concealed zip foot on your sewing machine makes sewing simple – the foot has two grooves that help to guide the needle in the right position. It is possible to use a regular zipper foot with the needle positioned over to one side, so don't rush out to buy a concealed zipper foot if you don't already have one!

Concealed zip. Concealed zipper foot.

Tip

To make the zip easier to insert, open the zip and press the coil away from the zip tape with a synthetic setting on your iron.

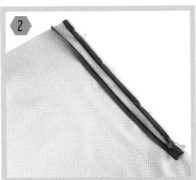

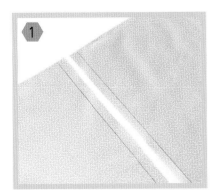
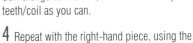

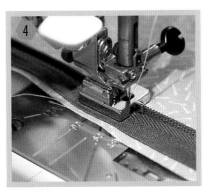

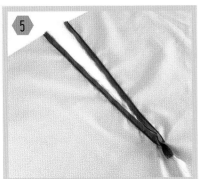
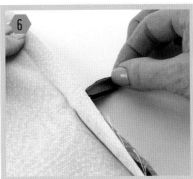

1 Mark your seam allowance on the wrong side of your fabric with an erasable ink pen – usually this is 1.5cm ($^5/_8$in), but do check your pattern instructions.

2 Take the left-hand piece of fabric. Place the coil of the zip over the marked line, right sides together. Pin, then tack/baste in place.

3 If you're using a concealed zipper foot, use the left groove to guide the zip coil through. Sew alongside the coil, as close to the zip teeth/coil as you can.

4 Repeat with the right-hand piece, using the right groove on your presser foot.

5 If you're using a regular zipper foot, open out the coil as you sew, taking the stitch line close to the coil. The zip will look as though it's twisted, but don't worry, this is normal!

6 Fold the two halves of fabric right sides together. Sew the rest of the seam from the bottom upwards, moving the end of the zip out of the way and matching the stitch line.

7 When completed, you shouldn't be able to tell where the zip ends and the seam starts... Until you open the zip!

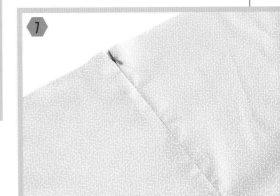

Inserting a lapped zip

This type of closure is used for skirts and trousers. The wider side of the seam slightly overlaps the narrower one, so that the zip is covered when closed.

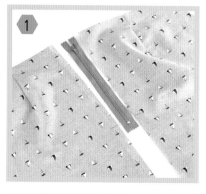

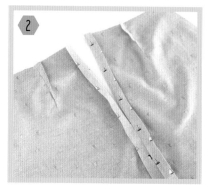

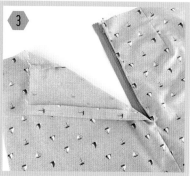

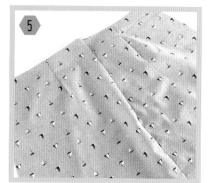

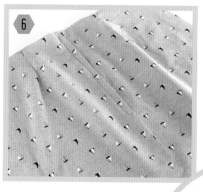

1 Mark the length of your zip on your fabric, just above the bottom stopper.

2 Sew the seam up to this point. Press the seam open.

3 Turn the fabric over to the right side. Gently roll the right-hand pressed seam back by 3mm (1/8in) and pin this edge to the side of the zip coil. This is what makes the fabric overlap.

4 With the zipper foot on your machine, sew along this edge. You'll need to move the slider out of the way as you sew.

5 When you close the zip you'll see how the fabric overlaps.

6 Pin the second side of the fabric to the remaining zip tape and sew, straight across the bottom of the zip and back alongside the coil to the top. Then press.

This is the finished zip closed.

This is the finished zip open.

58

Inserting a centred zip

This zip type is generally used for jackets and the centre-backs of skirts and dresses, with an even amount of fabric on each side of the zip coil.

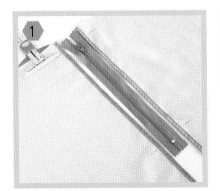

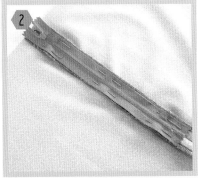

Use the zipper foot on your sewing machine to allow the needle to sew close to the zip coil.

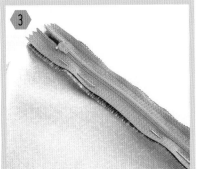

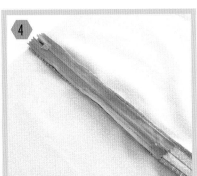

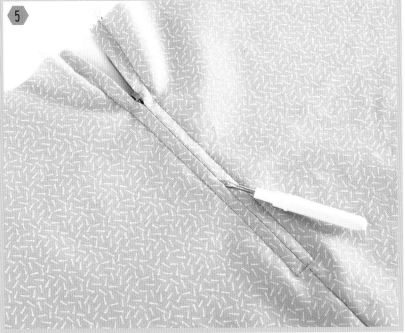

1 Finish your seams before inserting the zip – you won't be able to do this afterwards. Measure and mark your seam allowance from the top of your garment, position the zip so that the zip pull sits just below this, then mark just above the stopper at the bottom of the zip.

2 Set the zip aside for a moment. Sew the two pieces of fabric right sides together, taking a 1.5cm (⅝in) seam allowance; sew using a long stitch length from the top of the fabric down to the second mark, sew back and forth a few times to 'lock' your stitches, then shorten your stitch length and sew the rest of the seam. Press the seam open, then pin the zip, facing down, over the centre of the seam, before tacking/basting it (use a fabric glue stick instead of tacking/basting, if you prefer).

3 With the zipper foot on your sewing machine, sew one side of the zip tape to the seam allowance only.

4 Repeat with the second side of the zip and the other seam allowance.

5 Sew around the zip in a box shape from the front of your fabric, securing the seam allowances to the fabric as you go; leave the top unsewn for now. Use an unpicker to carefully remove the long stitches over the zip. When the zip is closed, the two sides of fabric will meet perfectly!

Project
TUNIC SWEATER DRESS

Update a plain sweater by adding details from a coordinating shirt! The sweater needs to have a wide bottom and neckline, as adding the shirt pieces will stop it from stretching. Add a longer length of shirt to make it into a dress.

Techniques

- Working with a slippery fabric
- Adding buttons

Notes

Use a 1.5cm ($^5/_8$in) seam allowance

You will need

- A short-sleeved sweater
- A coordinating ladies' shirt

1 Try on the sweater and measure the length you'd like to add to the bottom of it. Cut this length plus 5cm (2in) from the bottom of the shirt; I cut a 23cm (9in) length. My fabric is quite slippery, so I pinned the two sides together to stop it slipping as I cut.

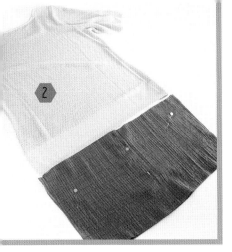

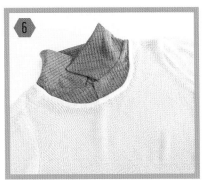

2 Trim the sides of the shirt evenly, all the way down to the hem, so that the shirt measures 2.5cm (1in) wider than the bottom of the sweater. Resew the side seams with a 1.25cm (½in) seam allowance so that the two pieces are the same size.

3 Turn both the sweater and shirt bottom inside out. Slip the shirt over the bottom of the sweater and pin, just over the rib around the bottom of the sweater, with the buttons of the shirt to the back of the sweater. Sew the pieces together with a 1.5cm (⅝in) seam allowance, removing the pins as you sew. Finish the top edge with either an overlocker/serger or an over-edge stitch on your sewing machine.

4 Turn the tunic sweater dress out the right way.

5 Cut away the collar and neckline from the shirt, in an arc shape that is around 5cm (2in) larger than the neckline of the sweater.

6 Push the collar inside the neckline, making sure it is sitting flat and even. Hand-tack/baste in place to keep the neckline flat before machine sewing around the sweater top. If you use the same colour thread as the sweater there's no need to remove the tacking/basting stitches. Trim away the excess shirt from the neck seam and finish the edge of the fabric.

7 My sweater had three small buttons at each side; I replaced them with buttons from the shirt to match the button showing at the back.

POCKETS

Here I will show you how to add patch and inseam pockets. The most important thing with patch pockets is to make sure they are securely sewn and, if you have more than one of them, that they are sewn on evenly! Inseam pockets may look intimidatingly professional… but once you know what you're doing they are really satisfying to create.

PATCH POCKETS

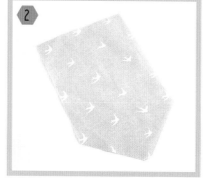

Patch pockets can look really neat on shirts, blouses and even pyjamas! But it is very easy to sew a wonky seam. Here's how to achieve the perfect patch pocket. Also take a look at the pockets on the Shirt Skirt project on pages 64–65.

1 Make a template of the finished pocket from card or stiff paper.

2 Place your template on your fabric and draw the seam allowances around it: add 5cm (2in) to the top edge, and add 1cm (½in) seam allowances to all other sides.

3 Fold over the top of the pocket twice by 2.5cm (1in), then sew.

4 Place the card template over the wrong side of the pocket, fold the seam allowances around the card and press. Here's a tip: a spray of starch will help the creases stay in place!

5 Remove the card. Place the pocket in position – pin if you wish, but I find it easier to secure the pocket with a fabric glue stick, so there's no manoeuvring around pins! Starting at the topstitch line, sew into the corner of the pocket then straight down the side. Continue to sew around the edge of the pocket, and finally repeat the triangle of stitches at the opposite side of the pocket. You may wish to mark these triangular lines first with an erasable marker.

INSEAM POCKETS

Pockets can be added to the seam of a skirt even if they're not included in the pattern, or to a shop-bought skirt if you feel it needs them! For shop-bought items it's unlikely you'll have the same fabric, so why not use a contrasting fabric to make a feature of the new pockets! Pay attention to the seam allowances, too, as these may vary.

1 If you're using a shop-bought garment, unpick the side seams. If not, mark where you'd like the pockets to sit in the side of your pattern pieces. Draw around the side of the garment on a piece of paper and make a couple of marks, 20cm (8in) apart, where the pocket will sit.

2 Place your hand over the template, in the position it would be inside the pocket, and draw a curve around your hand. Make sure the opening is 18cm (7in). This should leave 1cm (½in) at the top and bottom of the pocket for a seam allowance.

3 Cut four pocket shapes out of fabric: two pairs of mirrored shapes.

4 Place one pocket piece in the desired position, right sides together with the skirt front, then sew to the side seam with a 1cm (³⁄₈in) seam allowance (slightly less than the side seam allowance). Repeat with the other half of the pocket pair, on the right side of the skirt back.

5 Press each pocket piece away from the garment fabric, then topstitch along the seam inside the seam allowance to help the finished pocket stay in place.

6 Place the skirt front and back pieces right sides together, matching the top and bottom of the pockets. Sew the skirt side seam with a 1.5cm (⁵⁄₈in) seam allowance; sew down the side seam, pivot into the pocket and sew around the perimeter, then pivot again before sewing the remainder of the side seam.

7 Push the pocket inside the seam and press. Repeat for the other pocket pair on the other side of the garment.

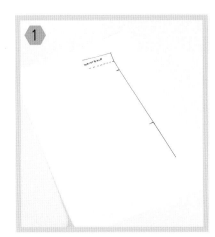

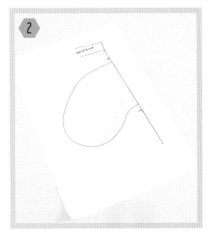

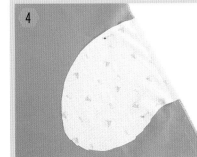

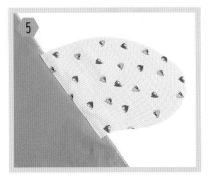

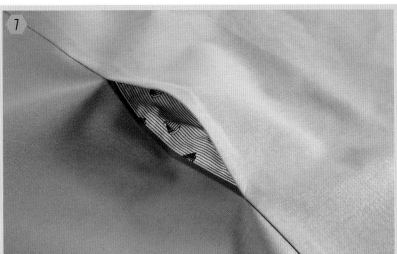

Project
SHIRT SKIRT

This skirt transformation is given a professional finish with the buttoned waistband – make sure you retrieve all the remaining buttons before discarding the surplus fabric!

Techniques

⊕ Gathering
⊕ Adding pockets
⊕ Button placement

You will need

⊕ A man's shirt, comfortably large enough to wear
⊕ Fusible interfacing (see step 3 to calculate the amount)

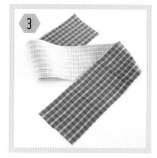

1 Cut straight across the shirt under the arms, then along the seams where the sleeves meet the body of the shirt.

2 Cut the cuffs off the sleeves, then cut along the seams to open the fabric out flat. Press.

3 Measure your waist, then add 2.5cm (1in) for seam allowances (decide whether you want the skirt to sit high around your waist, or low on your hips). Also measure the overlap on the skirt for the button front and add this. Cut a length of fabric from the sleeves to this measurement by 10cm (4in) wide – you'll have to join a couple of pieces together. Fuse interfacing to the wrong side.

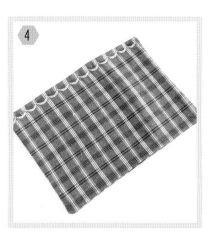

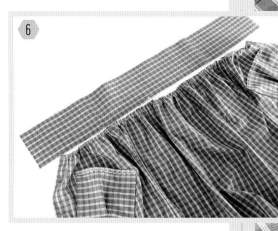

4 For the pockets, cut four pieces of fabric from the sleeves, each measuring 18 x 14cm (7 x 5½in). Sew right sides together in pairs, leaving a turning gap in the bottoms of about 4cm (1½in). Snip across the corners, turn right side out and press. Edge stitch across the top – I used a decorative scallop stitch on my sewing machine.

5 Pin the pockets evenly to each side of the front of the skirt with a little pleat in the bottom centre to give them some shape; I placed mine at a slight angle. Sew them in place around the sides and bottom.

6 Make two rows of long stitches around the top of the skirt, using your sewing machine. Pull gently to evenly gather, until the skirt top measures 1.25cm (½in) shorter than the waistband at each end.

7 Sew the waistband right sides together to the gathered skirt top, leaving the extra 1.25cm (½in) of the waistband free at each end. Fold the long raw edge of the waistband over by 5mm (¼in) and press. Fold the band in half right sides together (as shown) and sew the short ends.

8 Turn the waistband right side out. With the gathered skirt sandwiched between the two sides of the waistband, sew along the seam.

9 Button up the skirt and mark the position of a buttonhole and button on the waistband before sewing. One final press and you're finished!

Project
OLD TO NEW
JOGGERS

If you already own the perfect pair of joggers, but they are getting a little past their best, why not deconstruct and then re-make them? You know the shape and the fit are right, so what better way to make the most of them?

Techniques

- Deconstructing a garment
- Sewing an inseam pocket
- Adding an elastic waistband

Notes

Use a 1.5cm (⅝in) seam allowance

You will need

- A worn-out pair of joggers
- Jersey fabric – you may need to pick apart your joggers to calculate your fabric accurately; mine were UK size 10 joggers and required 1.5m (1½yd) of 140cm (55in) wide fabric
- 5cm (2in) wide elastic – measure the length by taking it around your waist and pulling to a comfortable tightness... I was hoping to re-use the elastic from the old joggers but unfortunately it was a bit over-stretched!

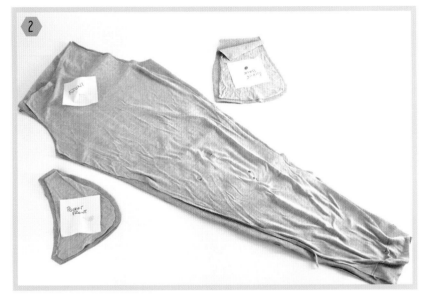

1 Take a good look at how your joggers are constructed; take pictures if that helps (1a). Your joggers won't be exactly the same as mine, so it's important to really study how they have been made. Make a note of any pleats, pockets or darts. Pin the darts and pleats in place now and mark the fabric to indicate their positions; you'll need to accurately transfer the positions to your new fabric. The joggers will be symmetrical, so you'll only need one half to make a new pattern from. Label each section before cutting along the seams (1b) to separate off one leg front, one leg back, the pockets and the waistband. By leaving one leg of the trousers intact you'll have a reference to how the pieces are put together if it gets a bit confusing later.

2 Unpin the darts or pleats so that the fabric lies flat. Use the dissected pieces as a pattern for your new joggers; if you've cut off the seam allowance from the old joggers, add this to your new fabric before cutting. Remember to cut two of each piece where necessary, on folded fabric so that the pieces are mirror images of each other.

3 Re-sew in any pleats or darts, using the marks you made in step 1.

4 Sew the front pocket pieces right sides together to the front of the joggers along the pocket opening only.

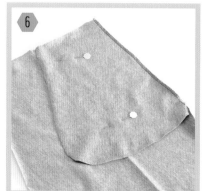

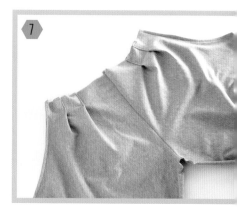

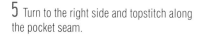

68

5 Turn to the right side and topstitch along the pocket seam.

6 Sew the back pocket pieces right sides together to the back pieces of the joggers along the side seams only.

7 Sew the front pieces right sides together along the centre seam. Repeat with the back pieces.

8 Sew the front pieces to the back pieces, right sides together along the side seams. Sew the pocket pieces together along the side and bottom edges; the top edge will be secured when you attach the waistband.

9 Sew the inside legs together, matching the leg seams at the crotch.

10 Take the waistband strip and sew the short edges right sides together to form a tube.

11 Fold the waistband in half wrong sides together. Slip the waistband over the top of the trousers with the raw edges meeting; pin evenly around the top. The waistband on my joggers is slightly smaller than the top edge of the joggers, so I'll stretch it to make it fit when sewing.

12 Sew around the top edge, leaving a gap of about 10cm (4in) in the back. Thread the elastic through the waistband – a safety pin will help – then sew the two ends of the elastic together, keeping the seam flat. Push the elastic inside the waistband and sew over the gap.

13 I decided to add cuffs to the legs of my joggers by cutting two pieces of fabric 20cm (8in) long and 1cm (½in) wider than the circumference of the legs. Fold each piece of fabric in half and sew along the 20cm (8in) side to make a tube (this is a similar technique to the waistband).

14 Fold in half wrong sides together.

15 Slip over each jogger leg with raw edges matching, then sew.

16 Turn over and press to finish.

SHIRRING

Shirring is a method of sewing with fine elastic thread in the bobbin of your sewing machine. As you sew in rows of straight lines, the fabric becomes ruched and stretchy. This is a simple, quick way of making summer dresses or gathering waists, wrists and necklines. The colours of thread available are quite limited, but the elastic is only seen on the wrong side of the fabric, so don't worry about finding a perfect colour match.

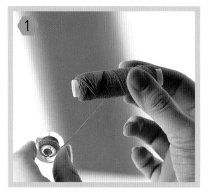

1 The elastic thread only goes in the bobbin, and you'll need to wind it by hand to avoid stretching. If you're shirring a large area you'll have to refill a few times, but it's worth it.

2 Pop the bobbin into its casing, as you would with ordinary thread. Whether you have a front- or top-loading bobbin, make sure you take the elastic thread through the tensions. Use regular thread in the top of your machine.

3 Increase the stitch length so that it's slightly longer than you'd normally use, and try sewing on a scrap piece of the same fabric you're using. The elastic should be quite tight, but not pulled through to the top of your fabric. Different machines behave in different ways, and you may need to adjust the tension slightly to get the perfect stitch.

4 Before shirring your garment fabric, hem or overlock the raw edge first, as you'll find this difficult to do after the fabric has gathered. Sew the first line of stitches with elastic thread and you'll see the fabric gathering up. Leave about 7.5cm (3in) of thread at either end of your work so that you can tie it off to secure. Sew the second row of stitches 1cm (½in) from the first, and gently pull the fabric straight as you sew.

5 Keep sewing in this way until the area you need is gathered. Knot the ends of the threads and trim. To tighten the elastic, steam over the fabric with an iron and the elastic will shrink slightly.

SEWING ON ELASTIC

Elastic can be sewn to a cuff on a sleeve, around the hem of a floaty blouse or around the waist of a dress to give it shape. It's available in many sizes and colours but generally isn't seen as it's sewn to the wrong side of the fabric. If you're sewing around a hem or cuff, sew the hem first, as you'll find it quite difficult to hem fabric after it's been gathered.

Mark the line along which your elastic will be sewn – this will help to keep it in a straight line as you sew. Choose a wide zigzag stitch on your sewing machine. Sew a few stitches at the end of the elastic to secure, then gently pull the elastic as you sew over it. It will help to ease the fabric from the back of the machine at the same time, but try not to pull against the needle or the stitches could become distorted. It pays to practise first!

To help you pass a piece of elastic all the way through a waistband channel – which can be a fiddly job – attach a safety pin to one end: you'll be able to feel it through the fabric and it will give you something to grip onto.

Project
SWEATER SKIRT

Tired of that sweater but love the fabric? It's so simple to transform a knitted jersey top into a chic pencil skirt, without the need for a zip. When you've finished the skirt, make a pattern from it so that you can re-create it from other fabrics.

Techniques
- Shaping a skirt
- Making an elastic waistband

Notes

Use a stretch or zigzag stitch on your sewing machine to prevent the stitches from breaking when you wear your skirt.

You will need

- An old sweater – a long sweater with no pockets is best
- 5cm (2in) wide elastic, cut to your waist measurement

1 Cut across the sweater, just under the armpits.

2 Finish the raw edge with either an overlocker/serger or an overcast stitch on your sewing machine.

3 Turn the skirt inside out and try it on. Pin down each side if it needs to be a little more fitted. Be careful when you take it off again! Make sure your pin lines are symmetrical (fold the skirt in half to check them against each other), then sew down each side using a stretch or zigzag stitch.

4 Take the elastic and snip off about 5cm (2in) – this will ensure that when the ends are joined, the elastic is tight enough around your waist to keep the skirt up. Sew the ends together, slightly overlapping, to make a loop.

5 With the skirt inside out, slip the elastic around the top and fold the top of the skirt over. Pin.

6 Sew around the top, just below the elastic, removing the pins as you sew. Sew over the elastic along the side seams to prevent it from twisting.

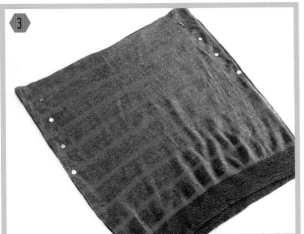

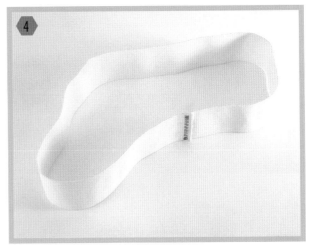

Project
WRAP SKIRT

This wrap skirt is simple to make and comfy to wear with its elasticated waist. Choose a floaty fabric such as viscose or polycotton to create a pretty drape from the waistband. The wrap should be sufficient to cover your legs and keep your modesty, but you can always add a couple of buttons at the side, if you want to.

Techniques

- Sewing in elastic
- Making a rolled hem (optional)

Notes

Use a 1.5cm (⁵⁄₈in) seam allowance

You will need

- The fabric you need will depend on your size: the width of your fabric needs to be 1.5 times your hip measurement, as this will allow the fabric to wrap around your hips and overlap at the front – you may need to join a few pieces together. The skirt can be as long as you like, but remember to add 2.5cm (1in) to the length for hemming
- 5cm (2in) wide elastic, cut to your waist measurement
- Rolled-hem foot (optional)

Measurements

- Place the elastic around your waist and pull slightly - use this as your elastic measurement
- Measure from your waist to the desired length of skirt
- Measure around the fullest part of your hips

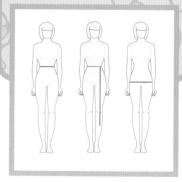

74

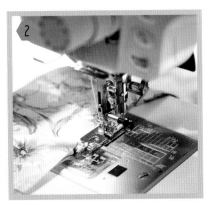

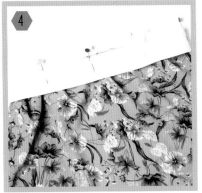

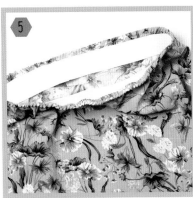

1 Carefully take your measurements and work out how large your fabric needs to be. You may need to join a few pieces together to achieve the right width.

2 If you're using the full width of fabric, remember to cut off the selvedges/selvages! Make a small hem along both side edges – a rolled-hem foot will help to create a tiny, neat hem. If you don't have a rolled-hem foot, create a double hem instead.

3 Wrap the fabric to create the 'tube' of the skirt; the circumference of the tube should be your hip measurement plus an extra 2.5cm (1in) to allow for comfort. Sew around the top to create the skirt shape.

4 Overlap the ends of your elastic by 1cm (½in) and sew them together with a zigzag stitch to make a loop (see step 4, page 73). Measure and mark quarter points around the loop with an erasable pen. Measure and mark quarter points around the skirt waist. Place the elastic over the right side of the skirt and pin around the top, matching up the markings.

5 Sew the elastic in place with a zigzag stitch, carefully stretching the elastic as you sew. Once it is sewn, fold the elastic to the inside of the skirt. Topstitch just below the fabric fold to hold the elastic in place, again, stretching as you sew.

6 Try the skirt on to check the length, then hem around the bottom; either make a rolled hem or a double hem.

Project
CIRCLE SKIRT

This cute circle skirt can be made for children or adults; for an adult size you may need to cut two semi-circles of fabric, depending on the width of your fabric.

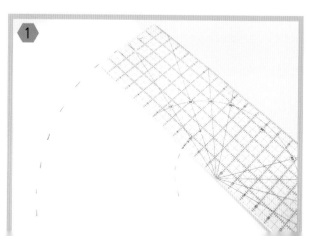

Techniques

⊕ Fitting an elastic waistband
⊕ Sewing a curved hem

Notes

Use a 5mm (¼in) seam allowance

You will need

⊕ Drafting or tracing paper, pen and ruler
⊕ Your fabric amounts are dependent on your measurements: you will need two squares of fabric that each measure your waist calculation (see step 1) plus the desired length of skirt; here I'm adding 9cm (3.5in) to 23cm (9in), which gives 32cm (12½in) squares
⊕ A piece of 5cm (2in) wide elastic cut to a length that fits comfortably around your waist

Measurements

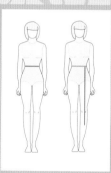

⊕ Measure the waist
⊕ Measure from the waist to the desired length of skirt

1 Take a piece of pattern paper and cut a right angle in one corner. To create your waist calculation, take your waist measurement, add 5cm (2in), then divide by 6.25. The waist measurement I'm using is 51cm (20in) plus 5cm (2in), which equals 56cm (22in), divided by 6.25, which equals about 9cm (3.52in). I've rounded this to 9cm (3½in). From the corner of the paper, measure and mark an arc with this measurement. Create another arc using the measurement you want the finished skirt to be, measuring it from your first arc: my desired length is 23cm (9in).

2 Cut out this pattern piece, then use it as a template to cut another piece 6cm (2½in) shorter for the top layer — you may wish to make this difference larger on an adult skirt.

3 Fold your fabric into quarters, then secure the larger pattern with clips or pins so that the straight edges both sit on a folded edge.

4 Cut around the pattern.

5 Repeat using the smaller pattern. You will have cut out two circles with holes in the centre.

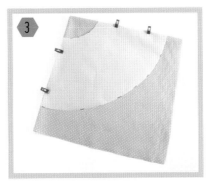

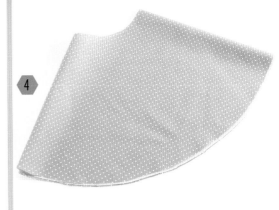

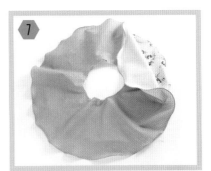

6 Hem both pieces around the outer edge; I found using a rolled-hem foot the easiest way to create a smooth hem.

7 Place the large circle over the smaller one, with the right sides of both facing upwards, matching the inner circular edges. Sew around the inner edge with a 5mm (¼in) seam allowance.

8 Push the larger piece through the hole to take it to the back, then press the inner circle seam.

9 Sew the ends of the elastic together, then open out the seam and topstitch either side to make neat.

10 Mark the four quarter points on both the elastic loop and the waist of the skirt. Pin these points together.

11 Use a zigzag stitch to attach the elastic waistband to the skirt, stretching the elastic as you sew.

Project
OFF-THE-SHOULDER TOP

Make this pretty top using your own measurements. The design could easily be extended to make a dress, or you could add elastic around the hem for a blouson! Don't use a fabric that is too stiff, or you'll find the ruffle will stand away from your body too much.

Techniques
⊕ Adding bias binding

Notes
Use a 1.5cm (⅝in) seam allowance
When cutting fine fabrics, make sure you have a large, flat area for cutting as the fabric can easily slip.

You will need
⊕ Floaty viscose; I used 127 x 112cm (50 x 44in) – see steps 1 and 2 for calculations
⊕ 5mm (¼in) wide elastic cut to slightly smaller than your shoulder measurement
⊕ Safety pin
⊕ About 60cm (24in) bias binding

Measure
⊕ Measure around your arms and shoulders where the elasticated top will sit
⊕ Measure your hips or the widest part of your body, divide by two then add 5cm (2in)
⊕ Measure your high bust, then from here to the desired length – this is your centre length

1 Cut two pieces of fabric using the measurement around your shoulders plus seam allowances for the width, and 30.5cm (12in) for the depth – this is your ruffle fabric.

2 Cut two pieces of fabric using half your hip measurement plus 5cm (2in) wide, by the centre length measurement (I opted for 48cm/19in long) – these pieces are your front and back. Measure 15.25cm (6in) from the top down each side, and 10cm (4in) in across the top. Cut a curve between each set of marks to form the armholes. This measurement can be amended later if need be.

3 Sew the side seams right sides together, then finish the seams as you like – I've pinked mine.

4 Try the top on to make sure the armholes are large enough – cut them slightly larger if you need to. Finish the edges with bias binding.

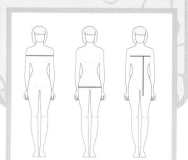

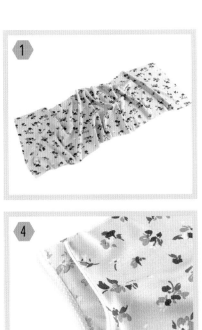

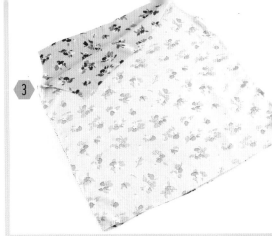

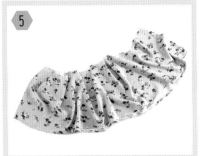

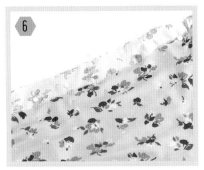

5 Sew the two ruffle pieces right sides together along the short sides to make a loop.

6 Mark the centre back and front of both the ruffle and the bodice with pins. Pin the ruffle over the bodice matching these points, with the wrong side of the ruffle to the right side of the bodice.

7 Sew the two pieces together along the front and back of the top with a 5mm (¼in) seam allowance. Fold the whole of the combined top edge over by 5mm (¼in) and then by 1cm (½in) to create a channel to thread the elastic through. Sew the hem in place but leave a small gap in the back seam for inserting the elastic.

8 Use a safety pin to help thread the elastic through the channel.

9 Sew the ends of the elastic together flat. Try on the top again to make sure it's tight enough – you can shorten the elastic at this stage. When you're happy, sew the opening closed.

10 Try on the top again to make sure you're happy with the length, then fold over the raw edge twice by 5mm (¼in) and sew to secure the hem. If you're adding elastic to the bottom, make this hem wider – as at the top of the blouse – so you can feed elastic through the channel.

APPLIQUÉ

Appliqué is the method of applying a decorative fabric motif – particularly fun if you're making children's clothes. This could be a hand-stitched felt shape, patterns cut from pre-printed fabric or fabric shapes you have drawn free-hand or using templates. There are many appliqué techniques varying in complexity, but for beginners, let's keep it simple.

Bear in mind you'll be sewing around the edge of your shape so don't choose a design that is too intricate – the outline of a hexagon is easier to sew than a tree, for example!

To make the application a bit easier, use a repositionable spray adhesive or fusible adhesive to keep the shapes in place.

1 Draw or trace your motif onto the wrong side of your fabric. If you're using adhesive sheets, fuse to the wrong side of your fabric, then draw onto the paper backing. Remember that the image will be reversed.

2 Cut out your shape and adhere it with spray glue or hand tacking/basting. If you are using fusible adhesive sheets, peel away the backing, place in position, then press with your iron. If you have trouble removing the paper backing from adhesive sheets, gently scratch the paper with a pin, then lift from the centre.

3 Shorten your zigzag stitch to a satin stitch for a dense outline which will stop woven fabrics fraying. A fine thread will work best: choose 60wt for a good result, and make sure you have a sharp needle in your machine. Set your machine to 'needle down' if you have that function, otherwise make sure that if you lift the presser foot to turn the appliqué, you turn the hand wheel to put the needle in the down position.

Tip
If you need to trim fabric back to your stitches, appliqué (or duck-billed) scissors prevent the blade from cutting through the threads.

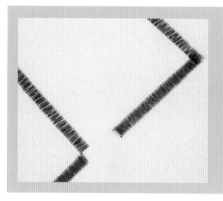

Tip
As a general rule, keep the needle to the right when pivoting; only move it over to the left if it's an inside curve or corner. The corner in the left of the image was turned with the needle in the down left position. The corner in the right of the image was turned with the needle in the down right position.

APPLIQUÉ EXAMPLES

I like the look of the simple blanket stitch on my machine — it gives a hand-sewn look to the work.

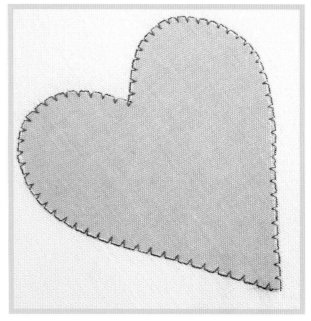

Try also using a blind-hem stitch if you don't want to see so much of the stitch. Always test out the stitch you'd like to use on scrap fabric to make sure you're happy with the look before sewing your project.

Felt appliqué looks charming when hand embroidered with blanket or running stitch. The depth and texture of felt really makes the stitches stand out. Try hand stitching blanket stitch around woven fabrics too — this gives a rustic look to your work.

Free-motion embroidery creates a charming hand-drawn finish, I particularly like to see the edges of the appliqué fraying slightly.

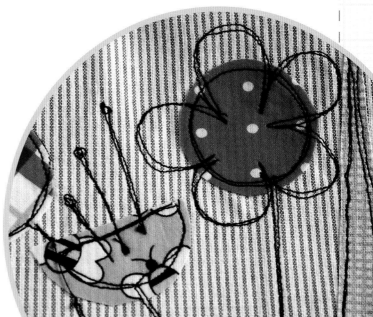

Project
CHILD'S SHIRT DRESS AND HEADBAND

This is such a simple make-over project, as the fastenings, binding and hem are carried over from the original items! There was plenty of shirt fabric left over to make a cute matching headband, too.

Techniques
- Gathering
- Appliqué

Notes

Use a 1.5cm (⅝in) seam allowance

You will need
- A long-sleeved knitted 3-year-old child's top
- A ladies' shirt

1 Measure 4cm (1½in) down under the arms of the child's top and cut across. Add an appliqué detail, if you wish (see pages 80–81).

2 Measure the length of skirt you'd like – mine is 38cm (15in). Cut this length from the bottom of the shirt, leaving the hem intact.

3 On your sewing machine, make two rows of long stitches around the top of the 'skirt', and pull gently to gather, evenly, to the same width as the bottom of the dress 'top'.

4 Pin the skirt to the top, right sides together and sew. Finish the seams to complete.

5 To make the headband, cut a strip from the leftover knitted top measuring 46 x 6.5cm (18 x 2½in). Sew the long sides together, right sides facing, to make a tube.

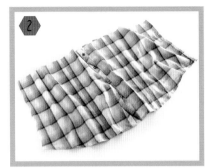

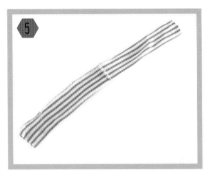

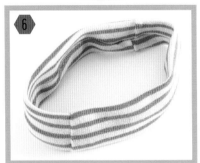

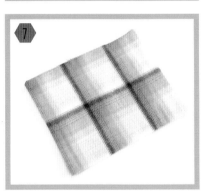

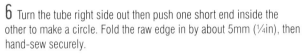

6 Turn the tube right side out then push one short end inside the other to make a circle. Fold the raw edge in by about 5mm (¼in), then hand-sew securely.

7 Cut two pieces of shirt fabric measuring 11.5 x 14cm (4½ x 5½in). Sew right sides together, leaving a turning gap of about 2.5cm (1in) in one side. Snip across the corners, turn right side out and press. Hand-sew the turning gap closed.

8 Take a hand running stitch straight across the centre, from one long side to the other, and pull to gather. Knot the end of the thread.

9 Cut a strip of shirt fabric measuring 7.5 x 5cm (3 x 2in). Sew the long sides right sides together to make a tube. Turn right side out, press, then topstitch along each long side.

10 Wrap the strip around the gathered centre of the bow and with the raw edge at the back, hand-sew to the knitted headband. It's a good idea to place the bow over the headband seam to cover it.

Project
BATWING DRESS

This dress is made from stretch jersey fabric so there's no need for zips or closures – plus, using my T-shirt as a guide means I have the perfect fit! The dress could easily be made shorter to make it into a tunic, or the sleeves cut straight for a more fitted look.

Techniques

- Drafting a pattern
- Making a neckline facing
- Adjusting a garment

Notes

Use a 1.5cm (⁵⁄₈in) seam allowance

You will need

- Fabric: this will depend on the size you are making – I am a UK size 12, and used 140cm x 2m (55in x 2yd) of soft jersey fabric
- A ball-point or stretch needle
- A twin needle
- Tracing paper for the pattern
- A T-shirt that is fitted but not tight
- A small amount of scrap paper
- A small amount of fusible interfacing for the neckline facing

Measurements

- Measure your centre back to the length of dress you'd like, then add 2.5cm (1in) to the length (it's better to be a little generous with the length as this can always be taken up later)
- Measure from the side of your neck to the length of sleeve you'd like, then add 2.5cm (1in)

1 You will draw out half a pattern and then use it to cut your fabric on the fold to create a symmetrical shape. Fold your T-shirt in half widthways and pin to your tracing paper. Draw a straight line from the neck to your sleeve length. Draw a 13cm (5in) line at the cuff, at right angles to the shoulder line. Extend the fold of the T-shirt to the centre back length. Draw in the curve of the batwing and the side of the dress by hand, tapering the sleeve into a curve under the arm, then flaring out to the hem. This can always be taken in later if you find the shape too wide.

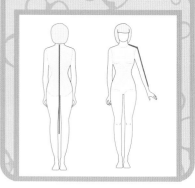

2 Draw two curved necklines following the shape of your T-shirt; the front will be slightly lower than the back.

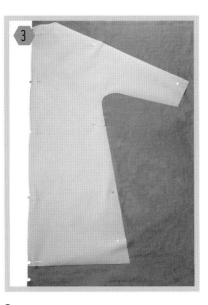

3 Cut out your pattern. Fold your fabric in half right sides together and pin the pattern along the fold.

4 Cut out the fabric, using the back neckline shape, to create the back of the dress.

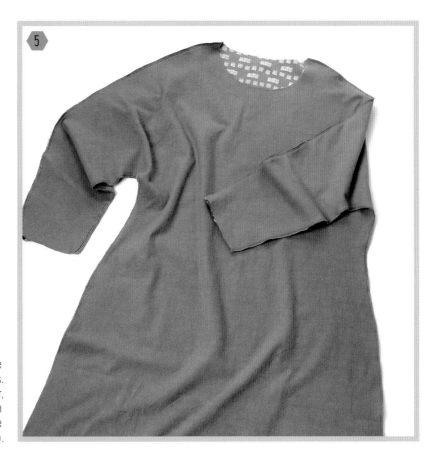

5 Repeat step 4 using the front neckline shape, to create the front of the dress. Sew the two pieces right sides together, along the upper arm and shoulders, then underarm to hem. Use the ball-point needle (see page 10).

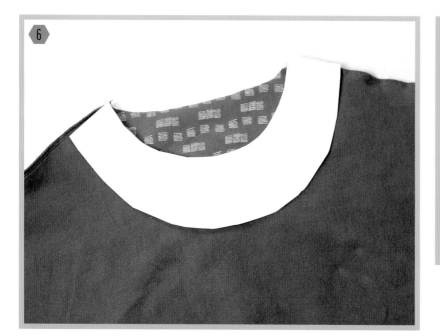

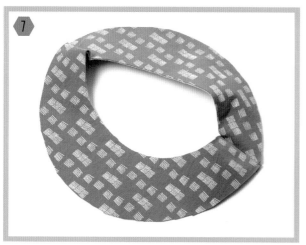

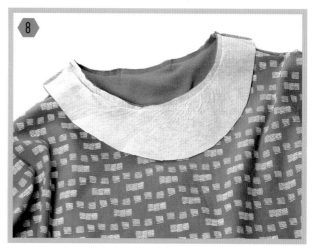

Check the fit...

Now try the dress on. Are you happy with the fit? You may want to take the sides in if you feel it should be a little more fitted – mark your new seam lines with pins before sewing, and check carefully that they are symmetrical. Is the neckline too high? You can also make the neckline lower or wider, should you wish, but again, make sure it is symmetrical before cutting.

86

6 With the dress inside out, trace around the front and back of the neckline onto paper and cut a shape about 5cm (2in) wide.

7 Cut these shapes from fabric, then fuse interfacing to the wrong sides. Sew the two pieces right sides together across the short ends. This piece is called a facing, and will help to give your neckline shape and structure.

8 Sew the facing right sides together to the neckline, matching the seams at the shoulders.

9 Turn right side out and press. Make a few stitches through both layers across the shoulder seams to hold the facing in place. You could also edge stitch around the neckline to hold the layers in place, if you wanted to.

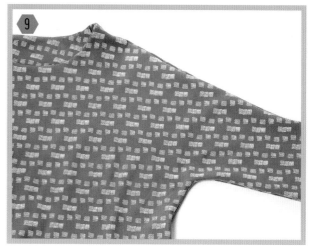

10 Fold the cuffs and hem over twice by 1cm (½in), press, then use a twin needle to secure them for a professional finish.

MAKE IT FIT

With a few simple techniques you can transform ill-fitting clothing into tailored items that really flatter your shape.

Before

After

ADDING DARTS TO A SHIRT

Loose-fitting shirts can easily be made to fit a little more snugly by adding darts. This shirt fits well on the shoulders, but I'd like to give some shape to the waist. (See page 43 for a little more information about darts.)

1 Try the shirt on inside out, or use a dress form if you have one. Pinch the dart positions on the back of the shirt and pin where you find it a comfortable fit. Don't worry about the darts being even at this stage. Pin the dart positions to the front of the shirt in the same way.

2 Take off the shirt (carefully!), then measure and mark the darts so they are the same length and width, and sit the same distance from the centre of the shirt. Take your time here to make sure you get it right. A French curve will help you draw accurate curves.

3 Sew, then press the darts towards the side seams.

4 Your shirt is now a flattering fit!

SHORTENING STRAPS

Do those straps on your favourite summer dress or camisole keep falling off your shoulders? Try shortening the straps a little...

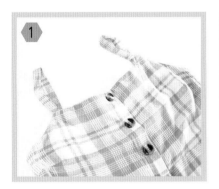

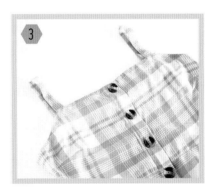

1 As with all alterations, take a good look at the way the straps have been attached.

2 Carefully unpick the stitches that hold the straps in place.

3 Pin the straps back in place making them a little shorter and pin, then try the garment on to make sure they're the right length. Sew in place.

Lengthening straps may require replacing them with a contrasting fabric or ribbon, unless you made the garment yourself and have some spare fabric; add a belt or matching buttons to bring the look together!

TAKING UP A PAIR OF JEANS

If your jeans are too long, or you just want to shorten them, but you really want to keep the faded hem, here's the way to achieve both...

Before

After

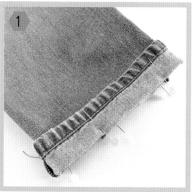

1 Measure how much you need to take up the jeans. Fold over by half the measurement, not including the hem: i.e. if you need to take them up by 5cm (2in), make the fold 2.5cm (1in) below the hem you're keeping. Pin and press.

2 Remove the pins and sew around the leg, just underneath the existing hem.

3 Trim away the excess fabric (this may not be necessary on a small hem).

4 Press the seam.

ADDING AN ELASTIC WAISTBAND

If your jeans are a perfect fit apart from a gape at the waistband, the quickest and easiest way to make them fit is to add a strip of elastic to the back of the band.

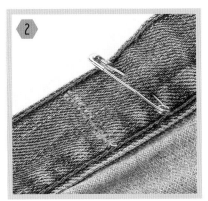

1 Cut a 20cm (8in) strip of 2.5cm (1in) wide elastic. Measure and mark 10cm (4in) either side of the centre of the back of the waistband on the inside, and cut over each mark, through the top fabric layer only. Attach a safety pin to each end of the elastic and thread through the waistband.

2 Pin one end of the elastic in place through the waistband and tuck the end inside the slit. Sew over the hole with a zigzag stitch in thread of a similar colour to the denim.

3 Pull the other end of the elastic to gather the waistband, remove the safety pin and repin it through the waistband to hold the elastic in place.

4 Cut off the end of the elastic, leaving enough to push under the slit. Sew over the hole with a zigzag stitch as before.

5 The join on the outside of your waistband will barely be visible, and you'll have a good fitting pair of jeans!

MEND IT

Don't despair if a much-loved item of clothing develops a rip or a tear, or even if the zip breaks. Give mending a go, and see whether you can fix the item, rather than just replacing it...

MENDING A HOLE IN YOUR JEANS

There are several ways to mend holes in jeans, so have a think about how you'd like the repair to look. You'll always see a 'scar' no matter how hard you try to make the mend invisible, so you might want to make a feature of it instead!

Darn it!

1 Small or difficult-to-access holes can be darned by hand.

2 Choose a strong thread as close to the colour of the fabric as you can.

3 Double the thread, and weave it over the hole and into the edge by about 5mm (¼in). Weave up, down and diagonally across the hole with small stitches until the hole is covered. The smaller the stitch and the more you make, the stronger the mend! Don't pull the threads tight to avoid puckering.

4 Your hole is repaired!

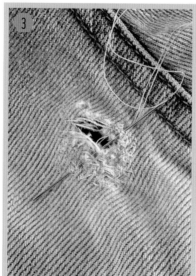
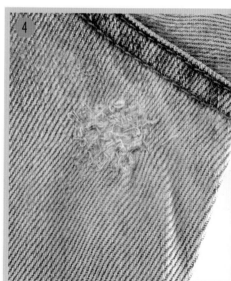

On the machine...

You could repair the hole in the same way using the darning foot on your sewing machine and free-motion embroidering over the hole – in this case, fuse a strip of iron-on stabilizer to the back of the hole to prevent it from distorting as you sew.

Patch it!

1 A hole in the knee can be repaired with a neat patch. You'll find it difficult to manoeuvre the repair underneath your sewing machine, so unpick the inside-leg seam alongside the hole by about 30cm (12in) so the leg can be opened out.

2 Trim the hole into a neat rectangle. Snip 5mm (¼in) into each corner.

3 Fold the edges of the hole to the wrong side of the fabric and press.

4 Place a piece of denim, as close to the colour of your jeans as possible, to the wrong side of the hole and pin. If you don't have the right colour denim, take your jeans to a charity shop/thrift store and match a pair from there — it's much cheaper than buying fabric! Sew the patch in place, then re-sew the side seam.

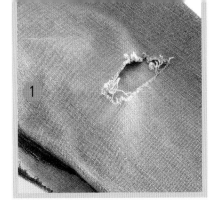
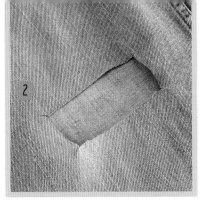

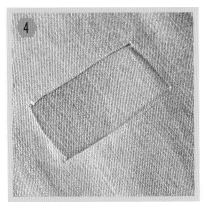

Make it a feature!

1 This is quite a small tear in the denim, but this technique would work for larger tears too.

2 Draw a shape, such as a heart, around the tear, then carefully cut it out.

3 Place a contrast fabric behind the shape and hand-sew with embroidery thread, using running stitch. If you prefer to machine sew, unpick the inside-leg seam as in step 1, Patch it! Scrub the raw edge of the shape to fray it slightly.

4 Alternatively, for a more handmade finish, place a piece of contrast fabric behind the hole without trimming, and secure it in place with hand cross stitches in the same colours as the fabric.

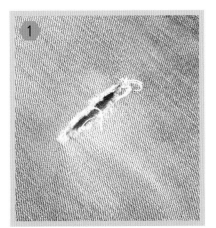
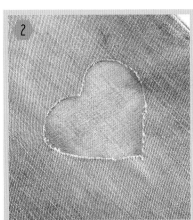

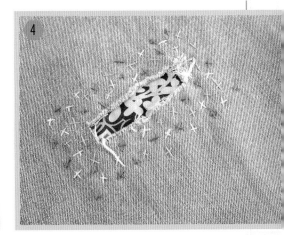

REPLACING A ZIP IN YOUR JEANS

You finally find the perfect pair of jeans... they fit perfectly and have been washed so often that the denim is beautifully soft. Then the zip breaks and it would seem this glorious, one-in-a-million relationship is over. Well, I'm happy to tell you that all is not lost, as that zip can be replaced!

On thicker areas, such as the waistband, your machine may need a little help, so if it struggles, turn the handwheel towards you by hand to help push the needle through the fabric. Use a denim needle, and try to match the colour of your thread to the original jeans thread.

1 The key thing is to take note of exactly how the broken zip was fitted. Study how it is sewn in, where it fits into the waistband and take pictures if you think you might need them to refer to.

2 Carefully unpick the stitches that hold the zip in place – be patient, as jeans are sewn with strong thread and there will be a few securing stitches (a bar tack) at the end of the zip.

3 Slip the left-hand side of the new zip in place, tucking the end inside the waistband. Hand-tack/baste in place with a contrasting coloured thread. You'll find it much easier to tack/baste instead of pinning as it's difficult to sew accurately around the pins. Sew the zip in place along the left-hand edge.

4 Repeat with the right-hand side of the zip.

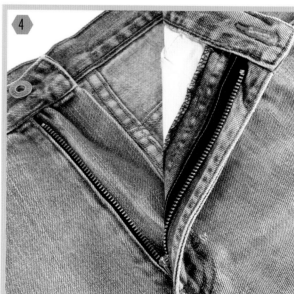

MENDING A TEAR

While repairing a tear in a seam is quite simple – you just need to sew over the original stitch line again, a tear in fabric is a bit more difficult to mend. You'll always be left with a 'scar' but there are a couple of ways of mending the hole.

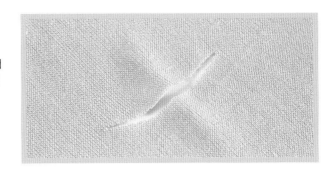

Using ladder stitch

1 Make a small stitch in one side of the tear, then take the needle directly opposite and make another stitch. Repeat along the tear – the stitches will look like the rungs of a ladder.

2 Pull the thread tight and the stitches will disappear!

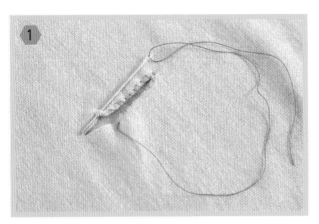

Using a machine darning stitch

This is usually used with a buttonhole foot, and the stitch goes back and forth to cover an area of about 2.5 x 4cm (1 x 1½in), If the tear is longer, move the fabric under the foot and sew again. Use tear-away stabilizer on the back of the tear to keep it flat, particularly on knitted fabrics.

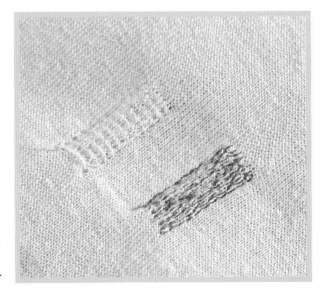

The thread used for the top repair is in the same colour as the fabric; the bottom repair is in a contrast colour so you can see it.

INDEX